"A dear friend in the faith, Jason has inspired me, and his desire to serve and love others is why he's one of the best leaders I know. Read this book and implement the lessons in your life. You'll be better for it."

DARRYL STRAWBERRY, eight-time MLB all-star

"For nearly twenty years, I haven't known a more sincere, dedicated, and values-based colleague than Jason Romano. His contributions to the unique culture at ESPN were deep and significant, and his observations in *The Uniform of Leadership* are striking and profound. Jason takes you behind the scenes at ESPN, sharing private moments with some of the biggest names in sports and television. There is great value in his journey, and Jason shares it generously. I urge you to accept his invitation to come along for the ride."

BOB LEY, Emmy Award–winning former host of ESPN's
Outside the Lines

"What I love about Jason is that he knows leadership is a daily choice, something so grounded in consistency that it becomes the root of who one is, in all they do. Jason has turned that leadership into a life of giving, serving, encouraging, helping, challenging, and equipping others to make an impact, to live a life fuller than they ever dreamed. We often try to box in leadership and what it looks and sounds like. Jason opens it up for all of us. I was thrilled to dive into this book, pull stuff out of it, and allow it to become part of my life and legacy."

DANIEL ORLOVSKY, ESPN analyst and former NFL quarterback

"A fantastic read! The lessons Jason shares from his seventeen years at ESPN are applicable for anyone. Whether you're a sports fanatic or a young leader hungry to learn from one of the best, pick up a copy of *The Uniform of Leadership*."

ADAM WEBER, lead pastor of Embrace Church and author of
Love Has a Name

"When I think of Jason Romano, I think of a hope broker and an arm lifter. His heartbeat is to help and serve others. This book will show you how to be more like Jesus with timeless leadership lessons and poignant stories from the sports broadcasting mecca that is ESPN."

CLINT HURDLE, former manager of the Colorado Rockies and
Pittsburgh Pirates

"As a former NFL player who now pastors a church, I appreciate the way Jason Romano intersects the world of sports with his faith in Jesus. This book has wonderful stories taking you inside the walls of ESPN and will encourage you to become a better leader."

DR. DERWIN GRAY, pastor of Transformation Church and
author of *The Good Life*

THE
UNIFORM
OF
LEADERSHIP

THE
UNIFORM
OF
LEADERSHIP

LESSONS ON TRUE SUCCESS
FROM MY **ESPN** LIFE

JASON ROMANO
WITH STEPHEN COPELAND

KREGEL
PUBLICATIONS

Published by Kregel Publications, a division of Kregel Inc., 2450 Oak Industrial Dr. NE, Grand Rapids, MI 49505.

Library of Congress Cataloging-in-Publication Data
Names: Romano, Jason, author. | Copeland, Stephen (Sports writer), author.
Title: The uniform of leadership : lessons on true success from my ESPN life / Jason Romano with Stephen Copeland ; foreword by Jon Gordon.
Description: Grand Rapids, MI : Kregel Publications, [2020]
Identifiers: LCCN 2020005005 (print) | LCCN 2020005006 (ebook)
Subjects: LCSH: Romano, Jason. | Sportscasters—United States—Biography. | ESPN, Inc.—Employees—Biography. | Leadership—United States.
Classification: LCC GV742.42.R53 A3 2020 (print) | LCC GV742.42.R53 (ebook) | DDC 070.4/49796092 [B]--dc23
LC record available at https://lccn.loc.gov/2020005005
LC ebook record available at https://lccn.loc.gov/2020005006

ISBN 978-0-8254-4639-9, print
ISBN 978-0-8254-7726-3, epub

Printed in the United States of America
20 21 22 23 24 25 26 27 28 29 / 5 4 3 2 1

CONTENTS

FOREWORD

JASON ROMANO IS ONE OF the best people I know, and I'm so excited for you to read this fresh take on timeless leadership lessons. In 2014, Jason and I connected on social media, and a year later he called me and shared his desire to do more purposeful work. I began to keep an eye on him and saw the impact he was making at the biggest sports media company in the world. I also watched as he made the leap from ESPN to a new opportunity that allowed him to expand his leadership platform and reach more people with his media expertise and broadcasting gifts and talents. Jason's unique way of living out his faith at ESPN, and now at his current job at Sports Spectrum, is empowering and inspiring. I discovered that wherever Jason goes, he influences others and makes the people around him better. He is a true servant-leader who loves and gives to others. That's who Jason is and that is what this book is all about.

In my time with Jason at various conferences, I've been impressed with his desire to share his story in a transparent and humble way. He tells his story in order to help you create a better story with *your* life. He shares his pain with a purpose, to help you grow, and he shares his wisdom, lessons, and experiences to help you make better decisions. I've spent time with thousands of companies, leaders, coaches, athletes, and teams, and this book is going to be a game changer in the locker room and in the boardroom. A lot of times, writers will share principles that they don't actually live. That's not the case with Jason and this book. In *The Uniform of Leadership*, he shares the principles he lives and how they can help you in your life and career. This book is one that you'll want to read, take notes on, and then give to someone else. It encouraged me, and I know it will encourage you as well. But don't just read it. Make sure you take action so the words on the page will help you create the life and career that you want.

JON GORDON,
best-selling author of *The Power of Positive Leadership*
and *The Carpenter*

INTRODUCTION

I LEARNED A LOT DURING my seventeen years working at ESPN. About journalism and media. About business and sports. But also about leadership, faith, and, ultimately, what true success really means in a world where people's definition of success has become convoluted with ego, materialism, and perception.

As much as I grew vocationally and professionally at ESPN, learning the ins and outs of the sports media industry, I also grew a lot personally. And, since I'm a man of faith, there were many days there that impacted me on a deep, interior, soul level. Days that touched me emotionally, mentally, and spiritually. Days that inspired me to be a better father, husband, leader, and friend. Days where it felt like God was using an experience with a guest or a boss or a cafeteria lady or a colleague to meet me where I was in my own struggles in life. Simply put, my experiences during my seventeen years at ESPN largely made me into the man, husband, and father I am today. It was there that I learned how to be a leader. It was there that I developed and evolved, confronted my insecurities and immaturity, and learned how to manage my ego and awaken my soul. As you know, personal development and evolution is a lifelong journey, but it was my time at ESPN that started me on that journey and inspired me to lead.

It is an honor to be able to share those experiences with you through this book. I hope these snapshots of my time at ESPN not only are engaging and entertaining—as many of the people in these stories are world-renowned athletes, coaches, or broadcasters—but will also inspire you on an interior level. I hope they motivate you to lead in a selfless and meaningful way. The people I've written about helped me on my spiritual journey, but my number one example for loving, leading, and serving is the Lord himself. I hope these examples of leadership help you create a healthy culture in your world and prod you to ask yourself the hard questions and confront your blind spots.

These experiences spoke to me and challenged me in unique and often uncomfortable ways. I hope they speak to you as well. May the principles in this book help you to do the job God has given you—to put on the uniform and play the position you're in, investing yourself freely in the team around you, whoever that is, wherever you are. Then you and they can win this life together.

You are where you are for a reason.

You are who you are for a reason.

I owe much to ESPN for the opportunities the people there gave me, and I'd be remiss not to say this book would not be possible without them. At ESPN, I got to meet my sports heroes—guys like Emmitt Smith and Darryl Strawberry. As a talent producer for over half a decade, I spent the day with some of the biggest names in sports and entertainment and guided them around campus to appear on a slew of ESPN's biggest shows. (We referred to these shows collectively as the "ESPN Car Wash," usually starting with *Mike & Mike* in the morning and ending with *SportsNation* in the late afternoon.) For someone who grew up as a sports-obsessed kid in the northeast, many of my days at ESPN felt like I was living a dream. But more than that, I was grateful to be surrounded by the best and most innovative leaders in the business. I worked every day for seventeen years surrounded by greatness.

A culture like ESPN's pulls you in and transforms you. It helps you awaken talents and gifts within yourself that you never knew you had. Pushed to the edge of your discomfort, you inevitably grow. You realize what you're made of when you're thrown into the fire. I was no one special for working at ESPN. I was in the right place at the right time, and while I focused on working hard and learning as much as I could, I also feel like I got incredibly lucky. I am eternally grateful for the opportunity; the values and environment at ESPN helped me step into who I could be as a leader.

ESPN isn't perfect. Like any big business, it has flaws and holes, areas with plenty of room for growth. But the company has been around for forty years, so they must be doing something right. I may not always agree with their decisions, but I believe the leadership at ESPN cares deeply about their employees, and they do their best to positively influence culture with their resources and platform. I always felt deeply valued at ESPN. And again, I am who I am today because of them.

My first book, *Live to Forgive*, chronicled my battle to forgive my alcoholic father. I hope you'll find this book just as vulnerable and transparent. I'm letting down my guard out of a desire to help you enter into your own introspection and journey inward. Just as I do not claim to have mastered forgiveness, I do not claim to have mastered leadership either. But I've learned a lot about both because of the life I have lived. In this case, I have learned a lot about leadership because of where I have been blessed to work. If I didn't share with you the profound lessons I learned at a place as cutting-edge and inspiring as ESPN, I would feel as if I were "hiding my light under a bushel." My experiences at the largest sports media company in the world were unique, transformative, and inspiring. I hope these stories will be the same for you in whatever leadership model you're in, whether you're a teacher, parent, coach, player, boss, or employee.

I believe that if leaders apply these lessons in the workplace, on the teams they coach, within the programs they manage, and in the projects they create, they can change our culture and our world for the better.

1

WEARING THE UNIFORM

HAVE YOU EVER CONSIDERED THE meaning and significance of the uniform that is worn by your favorite team or player? It might seem like a strange question because of the uniqueness of each uniform, but think about it. Every athlete's uniform is essentially the same. Sure, there are all kinds of different sports uniforms—baseball button-ups, football pullovers, basketball jerseys, and so on. Each team has its own style of uniform with different colors, a unique design, its own branded team name on the front, and its own font for numbers and players' last names on the back. But each jersey that a player or a team wears has the same significance and meaning. It will reflect three important things: the league, the team, and the player.

Consider an orange-and-royal-blue New York Mets uniform. Somewhere on the jersey, you'll see the age-old red-and-blue MLB logo featuring a silhouette of a batter, indicating the team's membership in the league—the larger whole. Without the MLB, the Mets don't exist. Though every team's jersey is different, all teams display the same logo someplace.

Second, the front of every New York Mets jersey displays the iconic diagonal "Mets" cursive or retro "NEW YORK" showing which *team* the player belongs to. Without the Mets, the player doesn't have a team.

Finally, the back of the jersey is personalized for the *player* with his last name and number (though some teams, like the New York Yankees and the Boston Red Sox on their home jerseys, do not show the player's last name). The player belongs to the Mets, which belongs to the MLB. Without the Mets and the MLB—a team to serve and a league to play in—the player has no larger purpose.

The uniform is a reflection of the way things are in the space where the player's career unfolds. Structurally, the MLB is of utmost importance. It is the entity that holds the league together and ultimately gives the player a paycheck. If the MLB folds, so does every team.

On a daily basis, the Mets are the most important. They are the context for the player's efforts on the field, whether for his coaches or his teammates, with whom he has personal relationships and is trying to win; or for the fans who watch him play; or for the city he serves.

Lastly, the player as an individual is also important, as it's his own attitude, effort, talents, skills, and unique gifts that lift up the team. But as vital as the most talented of players might be, he is nothing without the Mets and the MLB. If he is just playing for himself and not for a bigger purpose, he will struggle to fit within the structure. He will most likely feel lost, empty, and confused about his place in the world and his purpose in life.

The point of all this is that the very makeup of the player's space is others-focused. For the city. For the fans. For the hundreds within the organization. For the player's teammates and his day-to-day relationships. All of this is reflected on the player's uniform, something he wears almost every day from spring training through the late summer or fall.

Maybe you've never thought about what a uniform is communicating on a foundational level. But I bet you'd notice if, say, a player took the field with his uniform on backward so that his name was on the front. He would be a laughingstock. In our social media age, photos and videos of that player would probably go viral. He would stand out, and we'd think he was a fool. We all know that the player's team name is supposed to go on the front. And what if the player defended his decision to wear his jersey backward to the media? What if he said, "I did it because I believe *I* am more important than my team"? What would we think of him? Even more of a fool! That player most likely wouldn't play another game in a Mets uniform.

Why? Because the inherent design of the game is for the player to be *third* in the structure of things, as indicated in the systematic makeup of the league and communicated aesthetically through the player's uniform. For the team to thrive, exciting its city and its fans, the player *must* understand that as gifted as he might be, he must take the field each night with a higher purpose than to make himself shine. After all, when a team is losing consistently, the stardom of its individual players seems to matter less and less. Fans would much rather see their team win a World Series than a player bat .350 on the season. A good player might excite some fans, but a good team will ignite a city. A good team will get the whole country's attention.

And yet we live in a culture where people are metaphorically wearing their jerseys backward—or forgetting to wear their jersey altogether!—making their careers, callings, and passions more about themselves than about the greater good, more about a singular ambition than about serving the collective and doing something special with people around them. If the player makes his career about the name on the back of the jersey instead of the team name on the front, he will miss out on the best thing about playing sports and living life: relationships. Trying to accomplish something special alongside others.

▼ ▼ ▼

So, what is true success? If you look at Scripture, the Old Testament story of Nehemiah paints a beautiful picture in the third chapter of what true success looks like. Though the passage is somewhat obscure for modern times, detailing the rebuilding of a vital wall in Jerusalem, what strikes me most about the chapter is the frequent usage of the word *next*. It is used *twenty-six* times throughout the chapter in most English translations. Here is a snippet that reflects the nature and flow of the entire chapter: "The Fish Gate was rebuilt by the sons of Hassenaah. They laid its beams and put its doors and bolts and bars in place. Meremoth son of Uriah, the son of Hakkoz, repaired the next section. Next to him Meshullam son of Berekiah, the son of Meshezabel, made repairs, and next to him Zadok son of Baana also made repairs. The next section was repaired by the men of Tekoa" (Nehemiah 3:3–5).

I bet you've never seen Nehemiah 3:3–5 quoted in the first chapter of a leadership book before! When I started mapping out this book for the first time, I never imagined that the first three words from Scripture I would quote would be "The Fish Gate." It's easy for a passage like this, with its tongue-tangling names and hard-to-understand cultural context, to go right over our heads. But I love the themes these verses (and the entire chapter) highlight, and I believe we in our own culture can learn a lot from them.

The word *next* is used in two different ways throughout the chapter: to describe two people working alongside each other and to describe a subsequent task. Both of these notions go hand in hand.

In rebuilding the wall, it was necessary for people to work *next* to each other, tackling the task together, in order to move on to the *next* step in rebuilding the wall.

A DEEP SENSE OF TOGETHERNESS—OF RELATIONSHIPS—IS PIVOTAL TO MOVING FORWARD IN ANYTHING.

So what does this teach us about leadership? It tells us that a deep sense of togetherness—of relationships—is pivotal to moving forward in anything. As best-selling author and Storybrand founder Donald Miller once tweeted about experiencing meaning in life, "Let's choose to do something really difficult, something that saves lives, and let's do that thing with people we love."

Lots of people in leadership positions are attempting to do something really difficult. But few have the servant-focused approach to save lives in some way, and few have the relational approach of doing it alongside people they love. Lots of coaches desire to win championships and are committed to moving forward at all costs; lots of bosses desire to turn profits and grow their companies. But accomplishing these goals *next* to others with a heart for servant leadership and an others-focused disposition has largely been lost in our need (and lust) for results. Relationships have been neglected—on sports teams and in the workplace—in the frantic race to the top by those in leadership. The system is broken because people everywhere have their jerseys on backward, mistakenly thinking this life is all about them. As Rick Warren perfectly wrote in the first sentence of his best-selling book *The Purpose Driven Life*, "It's not about you." That maxim is the very foundation for true success.

▼ ▼ ▼

Before the 2003–2004 NBA season began, the Los Angeles Lakers picked up future Hall of Famers Gary Payton and Karl Malone to join Kobe Bryant and Shaquille O'Neal, two more future Hall of Famers and arguably two of the greatest players ever to play the game. The Lakers had won three NBA Finals in a row, then lost in the Western Conference Finals the year before, and were now loading up their roster for another Finals run. The entire season, however, was filled with drama. Not even the most accomplished coach in NBA history, Phil Jackson, could get his team to metaphorically put their uniforms on the right way and elevate the team over individual ambition. The Lakers were star-studded and veteran-laden, yet a public relations disaster and, to many, an embarrassment to the city.

Despite the toxicity in the locker room, the Lakers' talent alone was enough to scrape by on the court, finish second in the West during the regular season, and make a playoff charge, where they advanced to the NBA Finals to play the Detroit Pistons. But sheer skill could only take them so far. Though the Lakers were highly favored with their star power, the Pistons, who had no likely future Hall of Famers, absolutely manhandled them, smashing them in five games. The debacle led to the Lakers virtually starting over the following season, when they cleaned house, won only thirty-four games and missed the playoffs, and ultimately didn't make it back to another Finals for three seasons. They rebuilt their team around one of the greatest leaders to ever play the game, Kobe Bryant, whose love and passion for the game seemed to permeate every level of the organization and inspire all in their pursuit of excellence. Perhaps they no longer had a team as skilled and talented as the loaded 2003–04 roster, but their togetherness, cultivated by Kobe, ultimately led to back-to-back titles in 2009 and 2010.

Wearing your jersey backward takes you nowhere. It only fosters drama, discontent, and a culture of selfishness. It breeds comparison, greed, and a willingness to step on others—one's own teammates—in order to shine. Every once in a while, skill or talent might be enough to still take the team far and have a "successful" season (that is, if success is judged by wins and losses). But, as the Lakers proved, a team of individuals obsessed with themselves *never* leads to long-lasting success. It never leads to a dynasty. It never leads to a larger-than-life culture. It never ignites hearts and minds in a consistent way. Teamwork rises out of relationships—out of serving one another. It makes all the difference.

Of course, like many of you reading, I, too, was shocked on January 26, 2020, when the news broke that nine people perished in a tragic helicopter crash outside Los Angeles, including Kobe Bryant and his thirteen-year-old daughter, Gianna. The whole basketball world grieved. As a "girl dad" as well, so did I. In the subsequent weeks, we watched the world share story after story about Kobe Bryant. His legacy was less about the number of titles he won and more about his leadership—as a father of four girls, as a player who loved the game and inspired his teammates, and as a true artist and entrepreneur who was transitioning seamlessly into life after basketball. His legacy was about his relationships and who he invested in, and it offers us an opportunity to reflect. How will you be remembered? Will you be remembered as an others-focused leader, a teammate who made relationships and serving a priority?

▼ ▼ ▼

People in corporate spaces and in the workplace can learn a lot from the way things work in sports—all the way down to the very makeup of a sports uniform and everything it symbolizes.

No matter what you do, whether you're a CEO or a stay-at-home parent, an artist or an athlete, a salesperson or a plumber, each of us gets to wear a uniform every single day. It is just a part of life. We all represent something, whether we realize it or not. The way we live reflects our values. And we are all connected to people around us in different ways—through work and at home, through structures and systems, through friends and family. We each step onto the playing field of life, and we get to decide—every practice, game, and moment—whether our values, efforts, and passions will have a greater purpose; whether our skills, talents, and unique design will be reflective of our service for the larger whole: God and others.

Though I'm a Christian who has been deeply impacted by what has been communicated to us through the Holy Bible, I didn't write this book for Christians alone. So if the "God" word scares you, that's okay. The name of God has been used in a lot of manipulative and power-hungry ways throughout history. I can understand why that word might be scary; historically, Christians have sometimes gotten God horribly wrong. In fact, Scripture says that God *is* love. So when you read "God," you really can think "love." God connects us to one another and to creation and the world around us. God's love is the antidote to our broken culture. Love *is* the larger whole— the "league," if you will—the thread that connects each one of us and moves humanity forward.

But how many people show up each day on the field of life surrounded by others who are wearing their uniform backward, making everything about themselves rather than the good of the team—the family, the business, the church, their network of friends, and so on? This self-centered disposition is exactly why everything is so broken, especially in the workplace. And how many people wear their uniforms backward simply because that's what everyone else is doing—a trickle-down effect of selfishness? And how many forget to wear their uniform altogether, as if their belonging to the larger whole does not even matter?

What happened to the Lakers that fateful season seems to be happening everywhere these days. In the workplace. In the home. In sports. Our selfish and egocentric culture has infiltrated almost every avenue of life.

But it doesn't have to be that way.

▼ ▼ ▼

One of the unique themes of my time at ESPN was my involvement on the groundswell of a number of initiatives. What a blessing! I got my start booking guests for *Mike and Mike in the Morning* in their genesis, when they were only on the radio. After a few years there, I was hired as booker for *Outside the Lines* right when it transitioned to a daily television show. It was there that one of my coworkers, Melissa, created the first-ever talent-producing department, and I became one of two talent producers amid the thousands of ESPN employees.

See, back then booking guests at ESPN was kind of a cutthroat, Wild West culture where each show had to get its own guests. Crazy as it sounds, there was no department that centralized booking. Melissa had the wherewithal and foresight to create a department strictly for booking that came alongside the different ESPN shows, helping them get the guests they wanted. By the time I transitioned to another role, the department had grown to six people. I cannot tell you how special it was to be a part of a team that, though behind the scenes, was so groundbreaking. Suddenly, different shows could lean on the booking department or avail themselves of guests who were already on campus for other shows. Melissa had found a way to help everyone in the company by creating a cooperative environment. Many of the stories in this book come from those nine years as a talent producer, as I was fortunate to meet a number of athletes and coaches who were both fascinating and inspiring.

I'd like to say I always kept my jersey on the right way—even after taking charge of launching ESPN's NFL social media channels and working for *Mike & Mike*—but I can't.

During this seventeen-year journey, I at times wore my jersey backward. In the intensity and flashiness of corporate spaces, especially at a place like ESPN that produces shows on televisions and radio stations across the country and around the world, it's tempting to become obsessed with climbing the corporate ladder, getting the next raise, or earning the next promotion. It's tempting to go after status and accolades—to grab hold of what the world elevates, deems important, even idolizes.

My first book, *Live to Forgive*, took readers into my struggle to forgive my father and my journey of letting go. Now in this book, you'll witness my struggle with wearing my uniform the right way and my journey of awakening to what it means to be a leader and pursuing true success. I believe that, like forgiveness, this aspect of my journey is a reflection of most people's journeys. Many of us seek worldly success and status before awakening to what success is really about.

See, the word *uniform* has a couple different meanings. Both, I believe, are helpful when it comes to leadership, and both definitions are hard-baked into this book's title. The first definition is what we have already discussed: the garment a person wears. The second primary definition of *uniform* is when it's used as an adjective: "Remaining the same in all cases and at all times; unchanging in form or character."[1] For example, "A theme across the demographic groups at the polls was a uniform desire for lower taxes," or "The sneaker company, hoping to inspire its customers, implemented its uniform branding of justice and empowerment all around the world."

Why is this second definition interesting? Because even though the stories in this book are unique to my own experience at ESPN, each one has a theme that is a universal component of leadership. Though many of these stories are sports- or ESPN-related, they exemplify the uniform makeup of leadership in all aspects of life. In the home. In the workplace. In our personal lives. And, yes, in sports.

▼ ▼ ▼

I recently spoke to the students at Indiana Wesleyan University, a small Christian college in Marion, Indiana. One of their slogans jumped out to me; I was told it was a mantra in all areas of the university—in academics, in athletics, and in student life. It was three simple words: *I am third.* Just like a sports uniform, where the individual's name and number are on the back, ranked third in importance behind the league and the team, the uniform of leadership is for God to come first, others to come second, and us to come third. Each of those three is important. But if the order gets jumbled, then everything gets out of whack. The team breaks down; the company becomes steeped in gossip or drama; the church finds itself embroiled in a scandal.

I share this collection of stories, along with my own transparent reflections on where I went wrong in my personal pursuits and how I slowly awakened to the nature of true success, out of a desire to help us all re-center as leaders in a toxic, me-centered culture. I hope these accounts—about inspiring athletes with whom I had the pleasure of interacting at ESPN, and about some of the best leaders in the sports media industry whom I was honored to work alongside every day—will not only entertain you but also challenge you to refine your mentality and focus your heart on the right things. May you be inspired to wear your uniform the way it was designed.

PUTTING ON THE UNIFORM

Your uniform represents your belonging to a larger whole. Consider the implications. This belonging puts you in loving service of the greater good—your family, coworkers, teammates, clients, students, employees, congregation, your own sphere of influence, and ultimately God.

Those you are called to love and serve (which is everyone in your life) are not to be used as stepping-stones or mere mechanisms to make you shine. Just as individual selfishness rots a sports team from the inside out, a me-centered disposition will also rot your life. Despite the excitement of ego boosts and the rush of accumulating accolades, successes, or possessions, making your life about the name on the back of your jersey will ultimately be an unfulfilling and empty way to live.

In Matthew 22:36–39, Jesus was asked, "Teacher, which is the greatest commandment in the Law?" Jesus replied: "'Love the Lord your God with all your heart and with all your soul and with all your mind.' This is the first and greatest commandment. And the second is like it: 'Love your neighbor as yourself.'"

Jesus's words reflect the design of a kingdom uniform, and wearing it properly will ensure you play the game of life in the most meaningful, fulfilling, fun, and liberating way. The "I am third" principle is not about thinking less of yourself. After all, Jesus says you're to "love your neighbor *as yourself.*" It's difficult to love your neighbor fully, and to have a deep appreciation for him or her, if you do not love how God has made you and have a deep appreciation for your own life. Everything on your uniform indicates whom you are to love, but the ordering of those three things on your uniform means everything.

DISCUSSING THE UNIFORM

▷ Give an example of a time when a boss, employee, coach, player, or person in a position of leadership has worn their uniform backward or forgotten to wear it altogether. What were the effects on the team?

▷ Give an example of a time when *you* have worn the uniform backward or forgotten to wear it altogether. What were the effects on your life?

▷ Customize and personalize your uniform. What do you want it to say and to represent?

▷ What do you love about God, the people who God has put into your life, and the person who God has made you to be? Be specific here.

▷ What are two or three ways you can live your life today with more of an "I am third" approach?

2

BLOOM WHERE YOU ARE PLANTED

WHEN TONY DUNGY CAME TO ESPN in August 2010, he was promoting his second book, *The Mentor Leader*. Coach Dungy, the first African American head football coach to win a Super Bowl, had retired a year and a half before. His book was highly anticipated, as his first book, *Quiet Strength*, had topped the *New York Times* best-seller list right after the Colts won the Super Bowl in 2007.

I was excited to spend the day with Coach Dungy not only because of his book but also, on a personal level, because he was a man of deep faith. As an ESPN talent producer at the time, whose job was not only to book guests but also to take care of them throughout the day and guide them around ESPN to their different show appearances, I always looked forward to spending the day with a person of faith. This common ground often opened up the gates to deep conversation about life and purpose.

That's exactly what happened.

And it changed my life.

Joining Coach Dungy that day was a small entourage: his co-author, Nathan; his publicist, Todd; and his assistant, Jessica, whom I knew relatively well because we had worked on a couple projects together in the past. After Coach Dungy appeared on *Mike & Mike* early that morning, we were all in the green room getting ready for the next show. Jessica struck up a conversation with me about faith and life. Coach Dungy overheard us talking, and Jessica mentioned to him that I was a Christian too. That's when he asked me a question that would change things moving forward: "Jason, how do you live out your faith here at ESPN?"

Truthfully, when he asked that question, I had been experiencing a lot of doubt in my life about whether or not I should be at ESPN. I know that must sound crazy, considering I was working at the "Worldwide Leader in Sports" as a massive sports fan, performing a job each day that I absolutely loved. I can't even say that working at ESPN was my dream job, because the truth is that working at ESPN was *beyond* my wildest dreams. But since becoming a Christian nine years before, I had slowly begun to wonder if I was meant to work elsewhere. I felt like I was letting God down by working at a place like ESPN and thought that perhaps I needed to be at a church or ministry in order to truly serve him. I saw other people who seemed to be having more of an impact for the kingdom than I was. Out of my pride, I would often compare myself to others who seemed to be serving God more. I was struggling to wear the uniform I had when I thought maybe I was supposed to be on a different team. I was losing focus.

Overall, my life was compartmentalized. My faith was in one box, work was in another, being a husband was in another, and being a father was in yet another. If I was *really* going to live out my faith, shouldn't I work at a place that is about faith?

What I didn't consider at the time was that the man who asked me the question had lived out his faith for decades in the NFL and was now living it out in the sphere of broadcasting.

After thinking about Coach Dungy's question, I honestly said to him, "My faith is so important to me that sometimes I feel like I shouldn't even be working here. I feel like I should be working for a sports ministry like Sports Spectrum or FCA or AIA."

My response hung in the air.

That's when Jessica stepped between Coach and I and, with a stern look on her face and her hands on her hips, like a mother might look at her son who was late for dinner, she stared me down.

"What?" I asked, looking at Jessica.

"You don't get it," she said.

"Get what?"

"You don't get it," she said again.

"Okay," I replied, "what is it that I don't get?"

"Look at where you are," she said. "Look at the mission field here at ESPN. Look at the people you are impacting and those you will impact in the future. You need to understand that where you are, right here, right now, you are to bloom where you are planted. Until God calls you away—and he'll make it clear when it's time to leave—you can be a light right here where you are at ESPN."

▼ ▼ ▼

Though Coach Dungy's question changed my life, it was Jessica's response that met me where I was. Coach's question opened up the space for Jessica to step in and speak truth into my current situation. Her wisdom and boldness changed everything and sent me on a new path moving forward. A path that was more integrated and less compartmentalized. A path that was more expansive and less narrow. Thanks to Jessica, I realized that "Christian" and "ESPN employee" didn't have to be in two separate boxes. I could be a Christian ESPN employee, just as I could be a Christian husband and a Christian father and a Christian elder at church. I could be *who* I was, *where* I was, *for* others. I realized that I had neglected one of life's most fundamental truths: it's about relationships.

Jessica was right: Life was about thriving in the place God had put me. It was about being a team—willingly putting on the uniform (even if it's uncomfortable) and playing the role the coach had given me (even if that position is backup to the backup) until God opened the door for the next stage of my journey. The truths she shared helped re-center me for the next seven years. I continually reminded myself of the importance of accepting my team assignment: To build relationships with the people around me. To serve those I got to work beside. To let my light shine wherever I was.

Jessica reminded me of my identity, which rooted me in the present, which allowed me to think more about doing the best job I could rather than worrying about whether I was in the right place. She sent me on a journey of awakening to what it means to be the best me wherever I happen to be. That day was a catalyst that sparked difficult questions about leadership. How could I, instead of always focusing on the destination, lead people and be there for them right where I was?

I began to savor the little moments throughout the day that I shared with my coworkers. I became intentional in my conversations with those around me, investing in them beyond the workplace and allowing them to invest in me. I grew more outward-focused, more aware of people's needs rather than just my career. I became more present.

THE BEST LEADERS ARE THOSE WHO LIVE IN THE PRESENT AND LOVE AND SERVE THOSE AROUND THEM, RIGHT WHERE THEY ARE.

My reading broadened to include a number of leadership books[2] as I explored what it might look like to be a leader right where I was—my best me, right here, right now. The idea opened up a compelling new possibility: *Every one of us can lead through action and presence*—no matter what position we hold, no matter where on the hierarchical ladder we stand. The best leaders are those who live in the present and love and serve those around them, right where they are.

It's because of that day with Jessica and Coach Dungy that you are now reading this book that comprises leadership lessons I learned from ESPN. It's amazing what you learn when you put on the uniform of leadership no matter where you find yourself.

As a side note, I also learned it's okay to doubt where you are. It's okay to feel a sense of urgency to go elsewhere. For me, the doubts about being at ESPN eventually became a call to leave—to turn in one uniform for another. Seven years later, I felt that God opened a door for me to leave ESPN and join Sports Spectrum, a faith-based sports media company, and host a podcast that gave athletes and coaches an avenue to talk about their faith. But had I gone to ESPN every single day for seven years plagued with doubt about where I was, I would have been miserable and missed out on the many blessings God had to offer me at ESPN. I would have missed out on serving people right where I was. No one wants to work with someone who doesn't want to be where they are.

PUTTING ON THE UNIFORM

In a world where everyone is trying to go somewhere or do something, to climb upward or to build a platform, presence is key to leadership. In putting on your uniform, remember that you are where you are for a reason. That's not to say you can't have doubts or seek a new position, but don't forget, the people you are meant to love and serve—right here, right now—are of utmost importance.

Constantly thinking about the future and what might come down the line can remove us from all God has to offer—and all we have to offer others here and now. It can lead us to compartmentalize our lives rather than live in an integrated way. So honor the uniform you've got today. Throughout your life, you might change leagues or you might change teams. But the uniform you're wearing right now reflects where God has called you to be.

Discussing the Uniform

> ▷ Who are you? Why are you here? If your answer to who you are emphasizes hierarchy over relationship, consider saying it differently. For example, if you said that you are a "boss who is in charge of people," perhaps a better response is "I'm someone who tries each day to inspire others to bring out their best selves." If your answer to why you are here involves moving on—if it is destination-focused in any way—then again, consider a different answer. For example, maybe you answered, "To one day write and publish a book." A better response might be, "To enjoy creating and encouraging others with my words."

> ▷ How can you integrate who you are and why you are here into your day-to-day life today?

> ▷ What disciplines throughout the day can you implement that will help you to be more present where you are? Is there perhaps a motto or prayer that you pray throughout the day?

> ▷ What are the traits that you want to be known for? What can you do today that reflects those traits?

3

To Walk Beside or Climb Alone

THE IGNITION OF MY FAITH while working at a job so close to my heart changed me significantly. And that was good, because I had a lot of changes in my life and mindset I needed to make. ESPN took me on that journey.

Investing all of myself—my heart, mind, and soul—in the present has always been a struggle of mine. I am ambitious and driven. I have always been passionate about my work and my future. I have ideas of grandeur, and I love trying new things. I am always going somewhere new. And all of these are positive traits—until they begin to rob me of contentment. Until my ambition pulls me out of serving where I'm at and loving people where they are. When the destination I'm focusing on begins to negatively affect my mood and stirs up anxiety within me, misery and frustration are the result.

The destination mindset is especially prevalent in the corporate world, and ESPN was no exception. The hierarchical structure can tempt us to climb the corporate ladder all the more. At ESPN, the temptation was particularly intense because of the glamour and status of certain positions on shows watched daily by millions. Work, it seems, is often simply about moving upward at all costs. Receiving the next raise. Going after the next promotion. Getting the next title.

That day with Jessica and Coach Dungy, I had been struggling with integrating who I was with where I was. But at other times in my career, I experienced a different kind of destination-focused struggle: my obsession with where I wanted to be robbed me of serving and loving where I already was.

I learned how I had strayed the hard way. If you think being scolded in front of a Hall of Fame coach was embarrassing, just wait.

▼ ▼ ▼

I had a lot of professional growing pains in my twenties and early thirties. I thought my worth was found in moving upward. Today, people sometimes think my career was glamorous just because I worked at ESPN, but the truth is, my path was filled with lots of rejection. That only fueled my desire and ignited my ambition as a young man. Rejection animated my ego; I wanted to climb that ladder and prove I was competent, talented, and, well . . . *enough*.

I first applied for a job at ESPN in 1998. They called me in for a face-to-face interview, and I was like a kid in a candy shop. I couldn't believe I was where I was. I fell in love with the place. I was mesmerized.

I didn't get the job, but then I didn't feel like I had much of a chance, as I had very little experience in the radio industry. Still, I felt the year was a triumph just because I had an interview at ESPN. If I could ever work there, I felt, even making coffee runs, my career would be a success. I wish I had possessed this perspective years later when my ambition was running wild. It's funny how easy it is to lose perspective and take what you have for granted.

In 2000, I applied at ESPN again. This time I was much more qualified, having worked two years as an executive producer at WGY, a radio station in Albany, New York. Still, I never imagined it was enough to put me in the running for a position at so prestigious a place as ESPN.

I made it all the way down to one of the final two candidates. And since ESPN couldn't pick between the two of us, they created a brand-new position so they could hire us both.

But it was such a life-changing move, two hours away from our home in Albany, that my wife, Dawn, said ESPN needed to offer me a salary of at least $38,000 for us to even consider the transition. That was exactly the salary they offered. I'm convinced my wife called them and coaxed them into the decision, but she says she did not.

The move was a go.

I had somehow landed my dream job and didn't think I'd ever want anything else.

Then in early 2003, after working three years as a producer at ESPN Radio, I applied for a talent producer role on the television side. Once again, I made it down to the final two, but this time they didn't create a new position. They chose the other person.

Despite my employment at a place where I had long dreamed of working, I took the rejection hard. I thought my worth lay in what I did—in my title, status, and salary. I got caught up in the chase and climbing within the company. But after three years, I felt it was time for the next thing; like everyone else, I wanted to climb and was determined to move upward.

The next step didn't take long to come. Five months later, the same position was offered to me. I eagerly accepted it and suddenly felt validated. There—I had made it. I was working on the television side at ESPN on shows everyone was watching.

And, I admit, my attitude projected some arrogance, a sense

of "Look at me." What I didn't realize in my immaturity was that though my job title had changed, my role to make an impact had not, nor had my value. Whether I was working an entry-level position making $20,000 a year or was in upper management making six figures, none of it mattered if my self-worth was all tied up in status rather than focused on positively impacting people.

Then, ten years into my career at ESPN, I went after another position.

Like Icarus, I was determined to fly higher and higher.

▼ ▼ ▼

I was working as a talent producer for a show called *Outside the Lines* while also training to be a line producer. A line producer calls all the shots for the daily show. Think of that person as a sort of quarterback: commanding the field and making sure the offense runs smoothly. Line producers have people they report to, but when it comes to game time or on-the-fly decisions for the show, a line producer huddles everyone up, chooses a play, and tries to inspire the efforts of his teammates.

Being in training, I was asked to produce about twenty-five shows over six to nine months. Those shows were like getting called up from the minors to the majors. In my eyes, I was a full-time minor leaguer—a talent producer who booked guests for *Outside the Lines*—but once in a while I'd get called up to the majors to produce a show. And, like a minor leaguer playing in front of a sold-out crowd in an MLB stadium, I found the experience invigorating, electrifying. It whetted my appetite all the more to become a line producer and to keep climbing the ladder of importance. I *loved* sitting in the main chair. I loved the rush of it all, the risk, the excitement. If I'm honest, I also loved the idea of having that kind of influence at such a prestigious company. I became hyperfocused—borderline obsessed—with becoming a line producer. I wanted that position more than anything. I was determined.

The affirmation I received every time I produced a show only fueled my destination-focused mindset. I was told I was a "natural," I had "everything it took to be a line producer," and my "time would come." But here's where I made another error: in my compulsion to become a line producer, I began slacking in my role as a talent producer—the job title I currently held and the work I was paid to do. In focusing on the next prize, I lost sight of where I was. I was like a minor leaguer who started showing up late to practice with his minor league team the second he got called up for a game in the majors. Mesmerized by what my career *could* become, I once again got caught up in the chase.

My reality check came one summer, five months or so after first getting called up to periodically line produce, when I received the worst midyear review I ever received while working at ESPN. The words were haunting: "Jason is only caring about himself. His work is failing." I still have the note somewhere. I held on to it, determined never again to let myself become so obsessed with a promotion, never again to let myself lose touch with my current job title. Never again to let myself fly too close to the sun.

It was the wake-up call I needed. I realized I had unknowingly, over the years, adopted a "next thing" mentality. Blinded by possibilities, chasing a promotion with a new title, a hefty raise, and status, I had left my coworkers hanging out to dry. I wasn't present for the work I was getting paid to do. Instead, wearing my uniform backward, I was pushing ahead toward the job I hoped to get.

I reset my daily intention on being great right where I was as a talent producer. If the major leagues called me up for good, I would cross that bridge then. Meanwhile, I'd be there 100 percent for the team I was on.

▼ ▼ ▼

In our culture, we often obsess over when, where, and how the next door will open. Maybe it's a promotion. Or a purchase. Or a personal move. Regardless, thriving involves being present right where we are, investing in the process at hand. The best leaders aren't destination obsessed; they are present oriented. Yet in this country, most of us tend to become hyperfocused on the end goal concerning our careers, our relationships, our families, or our possessions. In so doing, we rob others and ourselves of our presence. The joy and potential of the here and now are lost, our heart gets left by the wayside, and we become hollow in our daily interactions with people we are called to love and serve.

THE BEST LEADERS AREN'T DESTINATION OBSESSED; THEY ARE PRESENT ORIENTED.

In his book *The Carpenter*, Jon Gordon's fictional character J. Emmanuel explains the difference between a carpenter and a craftsman: "A carpenter builds things. A craftsman creates a work of art. While most people approach their work with the mindset that they just want to get it done, craftsmen are more concerned with who they are becoming and what they are creating rather than how fast they finish it. After all, it's no use finishing something if it's not a work of art."[3]

When we are so destination-focused, we completely miss out on what we already have. We miss out on creating works of art wherever we are. I saw this on full display at ESPN when I managed our social media internship program in 2015 and 2016. My role was to interview interns, hire them, and work closely with them on various projects. In my conversations with many of them, often they would say something like, "I have this position now, but in four years I want this position, and then in five years I'll go after this position."

There's nothing wrong with setting goals, but sometimes it seemed the future was all an intern could think about. Constantly reaching for more bred fear and anxiety in their present circumstances, and that led to their micromanaging their future. Often I would think, "You've been an intern for three months; think about where you're at. Focus on where you are, be great where you are, and be thankful for where you are." (The irony, of course, is that I had the same tendency.)

One question I heard frequently from young interns was, "How do you move up at ESPN?"

"Listen," I'd say, "right now, you're an intern, and you're going to be doing work that isn't glamorous or fun. But you will learn a lot if you submit yourself to doing this kind of thankless labor now. If you are one of the few who get a job here, your first job won't be glamorous or fun either. You'll most likely be a production assistant who is essentially just in charge of the teleprompter, hitting the up-and-down arrow all day long. To stand out, you'll need to be the best teleprompter operator out there. It's boring, but again, if you do your best, if you're present with your work, you might get promoted to Production Assistant 2. And if you're not the best at that position, you'll have a hard time being promoted to Associate Producer."

I didn't need to say more; they usually got the point.

Ironically, in my own career, I later decided *against* becoming a line producer. While shadowing a coworker in that position, I saw that he was expected to work nights and weekends and had no say over his schedule. My daughter was four years old at the time, and I couldn't miss out on five to ten vital years of her life by being constantly on call at work. This was my catalyst for laying aside my status-seeking ambition to become a line producer. While there are family-focused line producers, I realized my desire to climb was not coming from a good place.

In *Lead...for God's Sake!*, Todd Gongwer discusses relationship-focused purpose through the brilliant metaphor of a jet plane. A jet plane's purpose is not just to get from point A to point B. If the plane made the trip a million times but didn't bring people to their destinations, it wouldn't be doing its job or fulfilling its reason for existence.

On every staff is a lower-level employee who believes he or she should be the boss. On every bench is someone who believes he or she should be a starter. But putting on the uniform you have—as Jessica taught me and as my midyear review revealed to me—is about being the best you in the moment you're in. It's about making your coworkers better even if you don't have the job position you want. It's about making your team better even if your coach isn't playing you as much as you'd like. Ambition need not be dampened nor goals abandoned, but each role you get to play is, first and foremost, an opportunity to serve others in a different way.

PUTTING ON THE UNIFORM

One reason why living in the present is so difficult is because the world we live in emphasizes moving up. People are judged by how much money they make, what they own, how many followers they have. Never in human history has perception mattered so much to individuals. Concern for how we appear, both to others and to ourselves, is amplifying the performance-driven narrative long extant in our culture.

So play different from the norm. Serve your teammates in the team you're on now, and don't get hung up on the future and all its uncertainties. It's natural to think and sometimes obsess about the future. Of course you want clear direction, and you long to experience the fruition of your passions. But don't let your angst about tomorrow divorce you from today—from the people and the task you are called to invest yourself in right now. The best leaders live in the moment and do their best to serve right where they are.

DISCUSSING THE UNIFORM

▷ In what ways does your angst or lack of clarity about the future distract you from what you are called to do right now? Why is it so difficult to wear your uniform properly right where you are?

▷ Think of a time when your "Icarus wings" melted because of your desire to fly higher and higher. What happened, and what did you learn from the fall? How did your new wisdom change things moving forward?

▷ Evaluate your life (graciously, without beating yourself up). If you received a year-end review from your family, friends, coworkers, employees, players, and so on, what would it say? That you are most concerned about yourself? If so, what steps can you take to change from a me-centered to an others-centered disposition?

▷ Reflect on today (if you are reading this at night) or on yesterday (if you are reading this in the morning). Dwell on the grace-filled moments—those moments you are thankful for—that you experienced with those around you. Consider why you are thankful for those moments. Spending time with them can help you, as a leader, see the depth and beauty of both the big and the small moments as they come throughout the day.

4

ROCK-SOLID AND SINKING-SAND IDENTITIES

WHEN JESSICA CONFRONTED ME THAT day with Tony Dungy, she did more than challenge me to bloom where I was planted. On a deeper level, she reminded me of my identity in Christ so I *could* bloom where I was planted. Because of that identity, I could be secure in the present even if I did not know what the future held for me.

Wearing your uniform the right way as a leader begins with having an unshakable identity. For me, that rock-solid identity is in my Lord and Savior, Jesus Christ. In my salvation, I am secure, whole, and unconditionally loved. Whenever I try something new and fail, whenever my expectations are not met, whenever I give my all and do my best in the pursuit of excellence yet am still met with harsh judgment or disappointment, I am challenged to rest in my unchanging, unshakable identity.

Without a strong sense of identity, it is almost impossible to be a good leader. A lot of people are poor leaders because they've constructed their identity—their house and internal home—on sand rather than solid rock (Matthew 7:24–27). When the rain comes down, when adversity hits, their identity collapses because of their fragile foundation.

An identity built on sinking sand in today's world usually involves clinging to or grasping for accomplishments and accolades. Such people often make decisions out of insecurity, ego, power, or desperation. It's easy to see when someone is projecting his or her own insecurities onto others—not an inspiring way to lead. We all know of people who care more about profits than about their co-workers; more about seeking status than about serving others; more about personal image than about people. That's a foundation of sinking sand: building on personal performance, the world's praise, materialism, and so on. Contrast that with building on your identity in Christ. That's solid rock. That's rooting your identity in a deeper reality that, transcending the manipulative ways of the world, traces back to love.

Almost every deep conversation I've had with an athlete, whether someone I was guiding around ESPN for the Car Wash or interviewing for Sports Spectrum, involved identity in some way. It is a hot topic of conversation because it's a deeply challenging concept. Many athletes struggle with constructing an unshakable identity. Why? Because there is such a major emphasis on their performance. Their entire career hinges on it, whether on the field, the court, or the course. The pressure to excel is amplified because of the hundreds, thousands, even millions of people constantly watching them. Kickers get cut because of a single missed field goal. Pitchers get bumped back down to the minors because of a poor inning. Players get booed by their own fans because of a single decision or mistake. Fantasy Football is a fifty-million-dollar industry, based entirely on individual players' performances.

Think about that. If an athlete's identity is built upon performance, he or she will most likely experience deep emptiness, unhappiness, and inner chaos. Because performance is a game that can never be won consistently; it will always be in flux, no matter how hard one strives to improve. That's why it's vital to construct an unshakable identity. Only on that foundation—solid rock, not sinking sand—can you build something meaningful and impactful to the people and the world around you.

▼ ▼ ▼

So how do you not only construct a solid-rock foundation but also build upon it, especially when the shadows of performance dog you in a world that is all about image and ego? A glowing example of someone who has done this her entire life is Jennie Finch, the world-famous softball pitcher who led the USA to a gold medal in 2005 and a silver medal in 2009. *Time* magazine described her as the most famous softball player in history.

IT TAKES AN UNSHAKABLE IDENTITY TO REMAIN INWARDLY HEALTHY AND OUTWARD-FOCUSED.

Jennie has had performance expectations looming over her since her youth, when she dominated the travel leagues. In college, success was her hallmark. One year she went 49–1 from the mound—absolutely astonishing, and unheard of today. By the time she started playing professionally and in the Olympics, people had come to expect perfection from her. That's a heavy burden to carry. It takes an unshakable identity to remain inwardly healthy and outward-focused when everyone who watches you not only expects you to win but is also surprised when you give up something as measly as a single hit.

Yet Jennie maintained focus on true success and what is most important in life: love, service, and having a positive impact on others.

I first met Jennie in 2009 when she came to ESPN to film a segment with on-air personality Jay Crawford, who was cohosting *First Take* at the time. Jay, for some reason, believed he could hit a pitch from her. He failed, of course. Most do. At the 2004 Pepsi All-Star Softball Game, Jennie famously struck out two future Hall of Fame MLB players, Albert Pujols and Mike Piazza, along with two-time all-star Brian Giles.

As exciting as the day at ESPN was, and as comical as it was watching Jay miserably fail on cable television, what stood out most to me was Jennie's friendliness and joyful attitude. It was apparent that day how very important relationships were to her. We had a softball team from a nearby high school in Bristol fielding balls that day (which required very little work, considering Jay's lack of contact at the plate), and Jennie went out of her way the entire time to get to know the girls and encourage them. You should've seen the way they looked up to her and how they would light up whenever she talked to them.

If you're not familiar with softball culture, you should know how much young American women look up to Jennie Finch. Jennie is a legend. My daughter loves her, even though Jennie's Olympic runs were long before Sarah began playing or watching softball. My daughter has had a couple opportunities to meet Jennie through different events at ESPN and Sports Spectrum, but each time she has said something along the lines of, "I just don't know what I'd do if I'd met her," and opted not to go because of nerves. I get it. But of any celebrity, Jennie would be the one to make a fan feel comfortable. What I saw of this spectacular athlete at ESPN was a woman who used her career of stellar performances not to lift up herself but to lift up others; not to build her own platform but to help others build their dreams. Jennie refused to build her life on the shifting sand of performance on the field. Instead she built it on the solid rock of her identity in Christ. And out of that identity—an identity rooted in infinite love—her life could flow out to others, inspiring and encouraging them.

About six years later, when Jennie spoke to our fellowship group of Christian coworkers at ESPN, to my surprise she instantly remembered me. I was used to reintroducing myself to athletes when our paths crossed again, especially high-caliber athletes like Jennie who meet hundreds of people every month. But she called me by name and recalled how we connected at ESPN. That might seem like a small thing, but to me, it showed not only what an incredible memory she had but also how aware she was of the people around her. She saw herself not as someone to be served because of her status in life but as someone who was there to know others and validate their efforts. My role in the events that day was a minor one, but good leaders don't see anyone as playing a "minor" role. They notice everything. They validate everyone.

▼ ▼ ▼

If you want to decipher what kind of foundation you are building your life upon, let your performance teach you where your inner work might need to be done. How your performance—good or bad—boosts or wounds your ego can reveal a lot. For example, if you don't become haughty after a good performance or despairing after a bad performance, it's likely your identity is beginning to reach beyond the evaluations of the world. This is a good thing. And a necessary thing. You begin to see the world as it is and become less desperate for its rewards.

A few years after Jennie spoke at the ESPN fellowship group, I was able to interview her on *Sports Spectrum Podcast*, and she repeated something she had told our group back then that reflected everything I always thought about her deep understanding of success. Standing on the Olympic platform during the medal ceremony, she said, she was reminded why she tried to live as she did—focused on helping others succeed, not on building herself up. The poignant feeling of emptiness upon achieving one of the greatest honors in sports confirmed to Jennie how important it is to live a life centered on loving God and loving others. Nothing else we pursue in this world will come close to filling the God-shaped hole in our souls. As wonderful as that Olympic moment was, it was also a window into the meaninglessness of obsessing over worldly accomplishments and accolades.

As King Solomon so poetically wrote in the first chapter of Ecclesiastes, "What do people gain from all their labors at which they toil under the sun? . . . All streams flow into the sea, yet the sea is never full. To the place the streams come from, there they return again. All things are wearisome, more than one can say. The eye never has enough of seeing, nor the ear its fill of hearing. What has been will be again, what has been done will be done again; there is nothing new under the sun" (vv. 3, 7–9).

Depressing though those verses sound, Jennie realized that day that they are also incredibly freeing. These wise words of the aged king, a man who had everything one could ever dream of in his lifetime, can free us from exhausting ourselves in striving, proving, chasing, and obtaining—from all our futile attempts to convince ourselves we are whole. We are loved by the God of the universe already. That's a strong identity—the only one that will last. Performances on the field will eventually sink into the sand. So will careers, accomplishments, and accolades. So will houses, cars, and possessions. It's no use building a life or an identity on any of them.

▼ ▼ ▼

My own performance has certainly been a window for me into areas of my life where I need to become better grounded in my identity in Christ. Publishing this book is a good example. My proposal was declined by almost a dozen publishers, and I found myself getting pretty discouraged and doubting the book. Should I write it, even though the idea came from my heart, from one of my passions in life: leadership? I began to doubt not just the book but myself as well. All based on others' feedback. It's crazy when you think about it. I allowed other people's opinions to discourage a project that was dear to my heart.

I did the same thing with my first book too. If you cannot tell by now, I'm an extremely ambitious and performance-driven person, and I had wanted to write that book for a while. Many people told me how it helped them on their journey of forgiveness. And that was what ultimately mattered: people's hearts were being changed for the better. Yet I let low sales and lack of awareness of the book discourage me. Sometimes my wife, Dawn, would ask me, "When will it be enough for you?" It's a profound question. When it comes to the paradigm of performance, it's never enough. There's always another mountain to climb. Another bigger, better speaking engagement. Another royalty report with higher profits.

As Darrin Gray and former Indianapolis Colts punter Hunter Smith describe in *The Jersey Effect*, there is a big difference between an identity built on importance and one built on value. They write: "What we're doing as a society is raising people who are very important. But they don't have value. Then, when athletes finish their careers, their importance is stripped away, and they don't see themselves as valuable. That's why we have the crisis we do in sports. That's why it's so difficult for athletes to retire. That's why athletes are notoriously in the news after their careers are over; they receive attention—whether good or bad—and that makes them feel important again."[4]

Importance comes from worldly success. Value, however, comes from love. This is vital to remember in a world with systems that revolve entirely around performance. It's why identity is so foundational, not only for athletes but for each one of us. While athletes' performances might be plastered on the front page of a newspaper or discussed by tens of thousands on social media in real time every Sunday during football season, most of us don't have such high-profile wins and losses. Yet whether we're a star athlete, a middle manager, or an automobile mechanic, society sets us up to be performance junkies. The American Dream is built upon the cornerstones of hard work and peak results, money and success. Even in education, a key building block of our society, students' performance on tests is more important than authentic learning.

Similarly, what's usually the first question people ask when they meet? "What do you do?" People view and judge one another through the lens of doing, not the lens of *being* who they fundamentally are—men and women made in the image of God and loved by God.

Don't hear me wrong. There is nothing wrong with doing. There is nothing wrong with performing excellently, to the very best of our ability. Working hard is a vital aspect of being a good leader. And measurements of performance can be valuable for gaining insights on certain processes or strategies. But performance becomes dangerous when it begins to dictate our health and happiness. The second my perceived performance in life begins to get me down is the second I know I need to open the Word, listen to a worship song, or remind myself of truths about my true identity in Christ.

My *value* comes from just one thing, and it's not how well I measure up by this world's standards. It's my identity as a child of

God. I am valuable because I'm someone deeply loved by God, as evidenced by what he did for me through his Son on the cross. That love, I hope, trickles down throughout all of my relationships and every facet of my life. With my wife and daughter, first and foremost. With my family and friends. In my job and in what I create. With my coworkers and the people I interact with daily. I want my hard work to flow out of that inherent truth of God's love for me— out of my innate value, not some messed-up drive to accomplish something in order to convince myself and others that I'm important. Whether you're a Christian or a non-Christian, I challenge you to root your value in love.

If you want to become a good leader, nothing is more important than constructing a rock-solid identity—or, better said, letting God and the truths in his Word construct a rock-solid identity for you. Once you do that, you can build a platform of leadership that, like Jennie's, is meaningful, encouraging, positive, and long-lasting. True success can only flow out of a true identity. Where are the cracks in your foundation? In what areas of your life can you feel the sand shifting or sinking beneath your feet?

▼ ▼ ▼

A decade after I first met Jennie, I posted a picture on Twitter of my daughter and me playing catch in preparation for her spring season. It was Sarah's second softball season for her school, and she was eleven and a half years old. Suddenly and most unexpectedly, I received a direct message from Jennie: "If you send me your address, I'll send Sarah some softball goodies. That picture was great. Easter blessings."

I was blown away. I had not reached out to Jennie, as I have sometimes done with athletes. She simply had the awareness to see an opportunity to encourage a young person, and *she* took the initiative to reach out to me. The last time we had talked, three years before, she called me by my name, and now here she was calling my daughter by her name. The best leaders have a way of validating others; using a person's name is one of the easiest ways, yet it's such a profound one.

I responded to Jennie, "Wow, you're amazing. Sarah is a huge fan of yours so this will be an awesome surprise for her. Happy Easter." I didn't tell Sarah about the exchange, but about a week later, a box arrived at our house. "Sarah, it says it's for you," I said to her, handing her the box. She opened it with eager eyes to find an assortment of softball swag: a couple Jennie Finch T-shirts and headbands, the book Jennie wrote about her faith-guided journey through life and softball, and an autographed photo of Jennie with these words:

SARAH, DREAM AND BELIEVE. GO FOR THE GOLD.
PHILIPPIANS 4:13.
ALL MY BEST,
JENNIE FINCH, USA.

My daughter was absolutely shocked. She had just received not only a bunch of softball gear from her favorite softball player but also a personalized, handwritten message from her hero in life. Opening that mysterious box was a moment she will remember the rest of her life.

That's what leadership is all about. So much of it involves having the awareness to create special moments for others. But you can't have that awareness unless your identity within is rock-solid. With insecurity, we become desperate, needy, and prone to tunnel vision. Instead of noticing the wants and needs of others and coming alongside them to empower them, we focus on our own interests and become frustrated when our expectations aren't met. With that mindset, you can give people what they want and have your motive still be all about you. People can tell, though. They know when you're giving to get and when you're giving to help.

There is no such thing as a selfish leader because selfish people aren't truly leaders, even if they're in a leadership position. Jennie is a perfect example of someone who, rock-solid in her identity, has the awareness to make special moments for people, even when she doesn't have to, even for people she doesn't know. Because she knows who she is, she understands that the real value of her platform as a sports star lies in building up others.

The photo featuring Jennie's note still sits on my daughter's desk today. And whenever Sarah sees the picture, she is reminded to keep dreaming, to keep believing, to take the necessary risks in life and go for the gold, and to do all of this because of her own identity echoed in Philippians 4:13, the verse Jennie cited: "I can do all this through [Christ] who gives me strength."

You, too, can take the risks and go for the gold in life—for the right reason. Not because you need to risk in order to go somewhere in this world. Not because getting the gold will somehow prove your worth. Do it because you are one with Christ and have already attained everything there is to attain in being loved by the creator of the universe.

PUTTING ON THE UNIFORM

Perhaps nothing is as vital in leadership as having a rock-solid identity. Without a strong identity and a dedication to constantly returning to your identity—all the truths about who God says you are, that you are loved and complete in Christ—you will always find yourself frantically scrambling around, looking for someone or something in the world to convince you of your worth. You must

construct your identity on something that transcends worldly success; otherwise, you are setting yourself up for failure.

You are more than your performance. You are more than what
you know, more than all your laboring beneath the sun, more than
what the world says you are. Continue to build your identity on the
solid rock of divine love, not the sinking sands of worldly success.
You'll be more outward-focused because your ego is less threatened,
so you can have the moment-by-moment awareness that launches
you into action as a servant-leader who creates special moments for
others.

DISCUSSING THE UNIFORM

▷ In your own life, what is the sinking sand on which you are
   sometimes tempted to construct your identity? How can you
   build your identity more on solid rock?

▷ In what areas of your life are you tempted to define your value
   with performance? What lies does the judgmental voice within
   often say about you? How can you replace what the world says
   about you with what God says about you?

▷ What are the fluctuating things in your life that make you feel
   important (for example: your career, quarterly sales, worldly
   possessions, victories, etc.)? How can you experience a deeper
   sense of unchanging value?

▷ How can you allow your unchanging value to spill out onto
   others? How can you instill values in others and create meaningful experiences for them?

5

LEAD LIKE TAMI

WEARING YOUR UNIFORM THE RIGHT way each day doesn't mean being in a perfect place that aligns with your passion, though it can unfold that way. It doesn't always look like climbing the corporate ladder or having a platform and influence as large as Jennie Finch's, though it can certainly include those as well. So what does it look like to lead right where you are?

When my coauthor asked me that question, a colleague of mine came to mind whom I saw almost every day for seventeen years straight. When I first started working at ESPN, I noticed her working as a cashier in the cafeteria. Almost immediately she started calling me by name. "Hey, Jason!" she'd say.

Oh, you remember me? It surprised me. I was brand-new and not at all near the top of the ESPN chain of command. But here was this woman in the cafeteria who knew my name.

I soon found out that Tami made it a point to know *everyone's* name at ESPN.

The cafeteria was heavily trafficked daily—after all, every person has to eat. And Tami, as the last line of defense in the cafeteria, made a unique impact on each person. Even on stressful or busy days when I had to grab a quick snack for an energy boost and return to the show I was working, Tami would make eye contact with me, call me by name, and say something about my day. It was as if she empowered me with her positivity and joy. It was subtle. It was brief. But sometimes the smallest things can make the biggest difference.

When we had more time to chat, she would ask me how my wife was doing—by name. She would ask me how my daughter was doing—by name. Obviously she was invested in my life, my work, and, well, me. Is anything more profound?

Tami might not have been in charge of anybody from a hierarchical standpoint, but it was more than apparent that she believed she could uniquely touch and impact everybody who crossed her path. She came daily and crushed her job. She spent every day serving others. Whenever I was flustered or running around helter-skelter, she would ask me, "How can I help you?" or "Can I get you something quick?" Whether I was in the midst of guiding a celebrity through the Car Wash or grabbing lunch with a twenty-two-year-old intern who was just trying to figure out life, she made each person feel like a million bucks.

In Tami's brief interactions with the hundreds who walked through her line every day, her smile, optimism, and desire to know as much as she could about each person was remarkable. Her positive outlook and cheer were contagious—even as she battled cancer.

Unlike most, including me, she never considered her job a burden, a drag, or a curse. You can tell when someone has joy at work, and if there is one word that describes Tami, it's *joy*. She was overwhelmingly positive and inquisitive. Not Pollyanna positivity but true enjoyment of, and gratitude for, where she was, what she got to do, and whom she got to be with.

Three things that epitomized Tami's leadership were positivity, a servant's heart, and investment in others. Whenever I get off track or feel restless and frantic in my pursuit of worldly attainments, I know that if I can get back to genuinely exemplifying these three principles, I'll get back to serving like Tami. I'll get back to wearing my jersey the right way. Back to contentment. Back to being present for others and trying to create an inspiring environment for them.

▼ ▼ ▼

It's no surprise that when Tami moved on to her next endeavor after eighteen years at ESPN, *everyone* noticed. On the last day of a person's tenure at ESPN, he or she is often given a gigantic six-by-three-foot banner with signatures and notes from their colleagues. Sometimes these banners just feature signatures from the big names as a sort of keepsake or memento for the time they spent there. Usually it's easy to find a spot to sign your name or write a sentence. On Tami's, however, the banner was jam-packed with *paragraphs* from people whom she impacted each and every day.

WHEREVER YOU MAY BE, YOU HAVE THE OPPORTUNITY TO INVEST IN RELATIONSHIPS WITH OTHERS AND LET THEM FEEL HEARD, UNDERSTOOD, AND VALUED.

Longtime ESPN sports business reporter Darren Rovell, who has since moved on to another media outlet, once noted that Tami's genuine caring made a difference for many people. Tami was a cashier in ESPN's cafeteria, but she did so much more than simply ring up purchases and take money. In each twenty-five second transaction, Tami showed authentic interest in each person who passed by her, and she offered a warm smile. Sometimes she would even tell you a little something about her life. Tami's position in the company did not minimize her positive impact on other people.

ESPN host Scott Van Pelt even dedicated his "1 Big Thing" segment on his show to Tami. He had this to say on air:

> There has been no more consistently kind and sincere presence in my time here than her. . . . She wears her smile like she wears a name tag, but she doesn't need a name tag because everyone knows her. She's battled cancer, and even that didn't wipe a smile off her face or dim her spirit or her warmth. When I saw that banner the other day packed with messages attempting to mirror the kindness she had shown everyone else, I wanted to tell you about her and brag about our coworker and our friend. . . . Our place will be less sunny because of her absence, and I get that you don't know her name, but she knows all of ours.[5]

In my humble opinion, Tami was one of the best leaders ESPN has ever had. She exemplified what ESPN is all about and what real leadership looks like. She gave me—all of us—an example to follow, every single day, for nearly two decades. By being present with others, by consistently investing in people's lives, by sharing her joy with those who came through her line, she left a mark—an imprint—on the hearts and minds of those she served and loved each day. She did it in a small way, but it ended up being a big way.

PUTTING ON THE UNIFORM

No matter where you are in the hierarchical order of the workplace, the locker room, or wherever you may be, you have the opportunity to invest in relationships with others and let them feel heard, understood, and valued. You don't have to be at the very top in the chain of command to have a profound and lasting impact on others. Don't overcomplicate leadership. Don't overcomplicate life. If you long to love, serve, and bless others, you are on your way toward leaving a meaningful legacy and, most importantly, helping others leave one as well. If you simply come alongside others and are truly present, you will impact people in a lasting way. Remember that Jesus was a mere carpenter and a poor rabbi with no place to lay his head—a humble servant born in a manger where animals fed, who rode a measly donkey on his "triumphal" entry into Jerusalem and died on the cross as a mocked king with a crown of thorns on his head. Yet he sparked a movement that changed the world—just because of how he lived and loved.

DISCUSSING THE UNIFORM

- ▷ How is Tami's legacy inspiring and challenging to you?
- ▷ What gifts has God given you in your individual design? How can you use those treasures to leave an imprint on the hearts and minds of others?
- ▷ When people interact with you, what would they say about the energy you impart to the environment you're in? Negative or positive? Mostly stressed or mostly joyful? Self-serving or others-focused? If you want an honest answer, actually ask those people or have someone else ask for you. Be gentle with yourself with the feedback you receive. We're all on a journey of becoming better leaders and awakening true success in our lives. Where is there room for improvement?

6

SETTING THE CLIMATE

AT ESPN, WHERE ALL OUR shows revolved around the news, one breaking story could change the entire workday and force us to toss all our well-intentioned plans into the trash. We could work hard to plan as much as we possibly could yet put none of those plans into motion because of the happenings of the day. That's exactly what happened the day when Seattle Seahawks head coach Pete Carroll came to town.

I was midway through my seventh year as a talent producer, in charge of booking guests for the ESPN Car Wash and spending the entire day with them, guiding them around campus from show to show. These were usually big-name personalities who, from a business perspective, were sure to boost each show's ratings. As you might imagine, this led to some interesting stories. Guests arriving at ESPN often brought massive posses. Some guests had egos that were even bigger. Many came to promote something they were passionate about and were high strung about maximizing every opportunity.

My role as a talent producer could be likened to that of a tightrope walker. Each day brought its unique walk on the wire; I did my best to minimize the tension and drama and help people feel secure in the belief I had everything under control. It was all about *feeling* out each step of the day, staying fully aware of my surroundings in order to avoid a catastrophic fall, and moving forward with confidence and intention. My high-wire dance entailed wearing all kinds of different hats. If, say, I saw that a guest was worn out, I might give the interviewer a time limit for questions or shoo off those hoping to grab a picture with the celebrity. Other times, I'd have to be blunt with the guest, or with his or her PR team, about how things needed to unfold if they wanted to promote whatever it was they were there to promote. I did what I could to set the room's relational and emotional temperature so everyone felt comfortable. Sometimes this meant feeling out the other rooms so I could adjust ours accordingly.

Once, a celebrity refused to go on a particular show because he didn't like one of its hosts. I tried to reassure the guest that the host was really nice in person and was looking forward to having him on the show, but he still refused. I had to inform the bookers at the show of the guest's demands. They then talked to the hosts, who ultimately told the guest's public relations team they didn't want him if he was unwilling to be interviewed by both hosts.

Another guest got frustrated that his segment on a show went such a long time. He left in a rage right after the show, missing the rest of his appearances on the Car Wash for the remainder of the day. Had his PR team told me about his time limit for each show, I would have communicated it to that show's bookers and played the bad guy to ESPN. But because they didn't, I had to defend ESPN and be the bad guy to the guest and his PR team. Still the blame fell on me in the chain of command for losing a guest who had been booked for a number of shows that day.

Things got even more chaotic whenever breaking news unfolded. Then the guest, who had likely cleared his or her schedule for the

Car Wash and traveled a long way to ESPN's campus, was suddenly at the mercy of the news. After all, viewers ultimately flip on ESPN for reactions to sports news, not to see celebrities or be entertained. At these times, my tightrope walk as a talent producer needed to be especially delicate and deliberate.

The day Coach Carroll came from California to Bristol, Connecticut, to promote his new book, *Win Forever*, also happened to be the day when the New York Yankees' legendary owner, George Steinbrenner, died. The news broke early in the day, after Coach Carroll had been on only one show, *Mike and Mike in the Morning*. Both of his big *SportsCenter* appearances were immediately canceled because ESPN went with wall-to-wall coverage of Steinbrenner's passing.

What struck me about Coach Carroll, a guy who was notoriously passionate on the sidelines, was his go-with-the-flow mentality. Not all his appearances got canceled. He was still able to appear on a college football show, since he had just finished coaching at USC, and on an NFL show, as he had just taken the head coaching job with the Seahawks. But the day was chaotic. Yet every time his schedule changed, he responded along the lines of, "No worries, whatever you guys need, whatever is best for you guys." He wasn't the least bit worried or upset. This allowed me, and the two or three people who came with him, to feel less worried as well. Coach Carroll, like all great leaders, was the thermostat that day, not the thermometer. Rather than reacting to conditions beyond his control, he set the temperature in the room and created a space for everyone else to relax and do their jobs.

I was inspired by Coach Carroll's reaction to the chaos that day, but when I published *Live to Forgive*, I became even more awed by the calm posture he had displayed. Driving to Albany, New York, to do a small media tour, I knew it wouldn't take much for my interview appearances to get bumped off the schedule depending on the news for that day. Publishing that first book had been a vulnerable experience, and I wanted the book to be a success. I found myself slipping in and out of wanting to control every aspect of the process.

Then I remembered Coach Carroll. Not only had he published his first book when he visited ESPN, but he had also traveled to us all the way from the West Coast to promote it. And he had done so during his only promotional window, in mid-July right between minicamp and training camp. Yet amid the day's disappointments, he had simply gone with the flow. What an example!

The best leaders don't become reactive or frantic when something happens that is outside their control. Coach Carroll treated the entire situation with grace. He understood I was doing my best to get him on as many shows as possible, and he was happy with what I was able to secure amid all the coverage about Steinbrenner's death. Because of his gentle, graceful response, the day ended up being a fun one for all of us.

▼ ▼ ▼

The apostle Paul exhorts believers to refrain from "grumbling or arguing" (Philippians 2:14). Such talk usually flows out of a fear of the unknown—we experience something unexpected and *react* to it. But being a good tightrope walker is about taking ownership over our own mentality. It's what I was required to do as a talent producer but which I sometimes struggle to do in my personal life. A tightrope walker who fears the wind will react to it frantically whenever it blows. But one who expects the wind to come will reconfigure his or her mentality, establish a new foundation, and approach each step with confidence. That tightrope walker continues to glide through the air, and everyone watches in awe.

Another way to think of it is in terms of the weather. It may be freezing cold and miserable, or the sun may be shining on a perfect day. Regardless, you can't control what's happening outdoors—nor can you control the outside forces that come at you during the day. Breaking news unfolds. People will let you down. Expectations won't be met. Things outside you will always happen, circumstances you can't change. If life unfolded perfectly every day, you wouldn't be on this earth; you'd be in heaven. What would truly be strange in this broken world is for all your high expectations to be constantly met.

But the good news is that, like a thermostat that controls the inside temperature of your home, you do have control over what happens inside yourself. Thriving requires a thermostat mentality.

And when you are able to set your own temperature, you can invite the crowd into your space and put them at ease, whether they are your coworkers, bosses, teammates, or coaching staff. It's up to you not to fall into the trap of simply settling in and being a thermometer who reacts to the outer pressure-cooker temperature. Instead, you have the power as a leader to confidently set your own internal temperature—to avoid overreacting, worrying, complaining. Maybe you can't control the circumstances, but you can control your response to them. Choose a godly attitude and it will ripple out to those around you. That's leadership.

I don't wish to downplay the real, legitimate frustration we feel when our plans blow up in our face. Neither am I out to drown passion or desire—the conviction that we want to work a new job, go after a promotion, or otherwise strive to advance. My goal, rather, is to share stories that help us rewire our mentality and determine, when we do not get what we want, to *still* wear well the uniform we've got. To *still* be thermostats even when things aren't unfolding how we hoped. To *still* give our all and be fully present, available, and approachable in our relationships with others even when our situations are not unfolding ideally. That's what thriving is all about.

Tami, one of the best leaders to ever grace the halls of ESPN, ultimately moved on to her next endeavor. Coach Carroll, at the ripe age of sixty-eight when this book was published, is arguably the most passionate and emotional coach in the NFL, as evidenced by his fervor and intensity on the sideline. There is no need to suppress what you are called to do or who you are. But as a good leader, it's important to remember that when you can't control your circumstances, you can control yourself.

▼ ▼ ▼

In my experience, *active patience* is what makes a thermostat mentality possible. It's what Coach Carroll practiced that day at ESPN. It's intentional patience. It isn't about putting a friendly smile on your face and acting like nothing is wrong. In fact, active patience often involves being deeply in touch with your own frustration or disappointment. It's okay for leaders to feel that way. What's not okay is taking it out on others. What's not okay is allowing the frustration to fester and lead to obsession or madness.

Active patience involves fully understanding the reality of your situation and still deciding to be a thermostat instead of a thermometer. Thermometers react in knee-jerk fashion and project their turmoil onto others. The best thermostats, in contrast, are so in touch with and in control of their own internal temperature that they can set the temperature for those around them as well. Consciously practicing active patience helps leaders become thermostats. Doing so requires introspection and awareness—asking yourself the hard questions, answering them honestly, and understanding the different aspects of your inner landscape.

Practicing active patience leads to personal growth and transformation. It's one signal of a leader's maturity level. More and more, I'm convinced that the best leaders are never impatient people. That's because the best leaders purposefully create culture: a temperature in the room that encourages people to thrive and unleash their gifts and best selves. A healthy culture won't emerge, though, when the temperature is constantly changing based on a leader's personal situation or mood.

Active patience is a daily discipline. As I write this, I'm in the middle of what feels like a continual morning saga with my teenage daughter. Occasionally she misses the school bus doing whatever teenage girls do in the morning to get ready for the day. My friends and family probably find it amusing to watch, but it frustrates me. As the person who works from home, I'm the one left with taking Sarah to school. But my calendar each day is planned and filled to the brim, and driving my daughter to school when I haven't planned for it throws off my day. Thank God it's almost summer as I'm writing this.

There have been plenty such days when I've been unable to contain my frustration and have taken it out on Sarah in an unhealthy way. Instead of the moment serving as a teachable one, an opportunity to help her grow and learn how her actions affect others, it hinders our relationship, manufactures guilt, and starts the day off on the wrong front for both of us.

The other day I woke up at quarter to six in the morning and saw that the lights were on in my daughter's room. The bus comes at six forty, so her early rising was encouraging. My wife, Dawn, and I spent time together in the kitchen before work. Time passed, but no daughter came down the stairs for breakfast. Fifteen minutes before the bus was supposed to arrive, still no Sarah. Another five minutes passed. Then another five. With each minute that went by, Dawn and I were becoming increasingly frustrated. And before long, the bus scooted by our house. Our daughter had missed it again.

I took a deep breath, calmed myself, and said to Dawn, "I honestly want to freak out on her, but that's not what I'm going to do when she comes down the stairs. It'll set a very hot temperature in the room and make things worse." Dawn agreed that we needed to control the situation and not react to it.

Our daughter eventually emerged at the bottom of the stairs and simply said, "Dad, will you take me to school?"

I paused and said, "Yes, of course, I will. But remember, you keep telling us that you want us to treat you more like an adult, and adults don't throw things on others last-minute. They're considerate to others. Had you asked me last night, I probably would have still said yes since I don't have any meetings this morning. But there are things you will need to think about as an adult."

She nodded affirmatively and said she understood.

Until next school year . . .

IT'S UP TO LEADERS TO CONSCIOUSLY PRACTICE ACTIVE PATIENCE THROUGHOUT THE DAY.

This might seem like a silly personal example, but my point is that it's up to leaders to consciously practice active patience through-out the day. Otherwise, they'll become reactive when things don't go their way. That doesn't mean we should ignore mistakes or set excellence to the side. A pushover, passive mentality doesn't set the right temperature in the room any more than a reactive one does. With no structure or consequences for actions or mistakes, the environment would become a free-for-all.

However, as Gerry Matalon, a former ESPN talent evaluator and one of my mentors, put it, "There's a big difference between cri-tiquing someone's performance and criticizing the performer." The former can inspire growth; the latter can tear down a person's value. It's your job as a leader to instill value in those you are leading.

In workplace environments and in team environments, reactive people often make those they are supposed to lead feel as if they have no value. Active patience helps create a temperature that positions others to grow, bloom, and thrive, thus moving the team forward and helping the growth process unfold smoothly.

PUTTING ON THE UNIFORM

When good leaders put on their uniform and take the field, they know they have the power and the potential to set the tone on the field and in the dugout, and they expect to do so. Good leaders realize they get to be the thermostat that controls the environment, not the thermometer that reacts to the environment.

Remember the infamous incident that occurred in the 2003 MLB postseason during game six of the NLCS between the Chicago Cubs and Florida Marlins? A fan instinctively reached for a foul ball headed into the stands and, in doing so, interfered with outfielder Moises Alou's attempt to catch it. Though Cubs fans scapegoated the fan, what might have actually led to the debacle that inning was the reaction of Alou and other Cubs players. Had they shrugged off the incident with a "well, that's baseball" attitude, the team might have been able to simply move on to the next play, remain focused in the moment, and close out the inning. They might have settled the fans down as well. Instead, many players got angry and bitter, and the negative energy in Wrigley Field rose astronomically (watch the ESPN *30 for 30* documentary "Catching Hell"). Players made errors and silly mistakes. In the end, because of the Cubs players' thermometer mentality, they gave up eight runs that inning and went on to lose the series and miss winning their first National League pennant since 1945.

In the spaces where your life unfolds, be a thermostat. Don't be reactive; be proactive. Take the initiative to set the tone. Bad things happen, and people make mistakes all the time—that's life. But you as a leader can choose to react to adversity the right way. Failing to do so could have long-lasting effects on your teammates' performance as well as those in your environment who are watching. But choosing to respond wisely can influence others positively in ways you can't foresee.

DISCUSSING THE UNIFORM

▷ Reflect upon a time when your reaction to something in life made things worse in the end. What did you learn from that experience?

▷ Reflect upon a time when someone else's reaction to circumstances, perhaps a leader's reaction, had a detrimental impact on the environment, making it unstable and shaky. What does that situation teach you about leadership?

▷ Think of a good leader in your life. How did his or her active patience help you or others grow, develop, and evolve?

▷ Whenever you are tempted to react to something and be a thermometer, how can you zoom out, calm down, and get back to being a thermostat? This discipline will be different from person to person. What are some practices *you* can employ that will help you re-center so you can lead with control and stability?

7

BENEATH THE SURFACE

WHEN IT COMES TO ACTIVE patience, I think of Jesus's parable of the growing seed: "This is what the kingdom of God is like. A man scatters seed on the ground. Night and day, whether he sleeps or gets up, the seed sprouts and grows, though he does not know how. All by itself the soil produces grain—first the stalk, then the head, then the full kernel in the head. As soon as the grain is ripe, he puts the sickle to it, because the harvest has come" (Mark 4:26–29).

This parable inspires me with its depiction of how things work in this world. Consider the kingdom of God to be what is happening on a deeper level in your life and through your efforts out in the field. If you're giving your all—doing your best in the present to be *who* you truly are *where* you are—then it's likely something beautiful and mysterious is happening beneath the surface. I say "truly" because a lot of times, especially in the corporate world or in athletics, we make decisions based on our ego or ambition—*not* on who we truly are. But if you're being your authentic self where you are—using your unique gifts to love and serve others, to be selfless and others-focused—then you are blooming, and you are planting seeds that will one day burst through the ground and bloom as well.

However, believing that this process is really happening can sometimes be difficult and even agonizing. That's because while you are preparing the seed and waiting for it to grow, you usually have nothing to show from your efforts. You're in the waiting phase. When nothing is sprouting through the soil, what are you worth?

That day with Jessica and Coach Dungy inspired me to dare to believe I was positioned right where I was for a reason and should invest all my energy in blooming where I was planted. The challenge in the coming years was *continuing* to do so even when I wasn't seeing the fruit I hoped for. I doubted my impact on others because I couldn't measure it. I was no longer chasing success in the eyes of the world or trying to move up the corporate ladder. I was focused on serving. But how was I to know if I was truly serving people or having a positive influence on them? Don't we all want to live purposeful lives? How do we know if we are really making a difference? I wanted to do so on a deep level at ESPN, but I also wanted to see the impact I was having.

At Sports Spectrum, I know the stats. We've had more than one million people download our podcast. I can tell you how many subscribers we have. I can tell you how many followers our social media channels have. All of this is validating to me. It tells me that hundreds of thousands of people are experiencing the faith-based content we produce, and it's reasonable to assume many are being deeply influenced.

At a place like ESPN, on the other hand, that impact was difficult to measure. You never know if you're making a real difference in the way you are living your life at your job. For some, like me, this can feel maddening. It's probably an ego thing. And it's a lack of trust in being who I know I am supposed to be and doing what I know I'm supposed to do.

In our culture, we are addicted to quick results and measurements to validate our efforts. We need data to prove that our direction is worthwhile. This isn't necessarily a bad thing. The data often is insightful and telling. But one thing it doesn't show is what is happening below the surface—the hidden workings beneath the soil after the seed is scattered on the ground. This can't be measured.

▼ ▼ ▼

On April 15, 2013, the Boston Marathon bombing devastated the city of Boston and shook many who worked at ESPN. Many employees are stationed in Boston, as Bristol is only two hours away.

I was sitting in my cubicle when I heard a knock on my sliding door. It was one of my colleagues, Charlie. I didn't know him well; we saw each other maybe once or twice a week in passing.

"Hey Charlie," I said, "what's going on?"

"Terrible what we're experiencing today, huh, Jay?"

"Yeah, it's awful."

"Hey," he said, pausing, "do you want to come with me into the break room for a second? I think we need to pray."

His request caught me off guard. As I mentioned, I didn't know Charlie particularly well. But I wasn't going to turn down a request like that.

"Yeah, let's go," I said.

Praying in the break room was not a normal occurrence at ESPN. The break room is a public place with people going in and out for, well, breaks. But for the next ten to fifteen minutes, Charlie and I prayed together in that room, lifting up those who were suffering and all the friends and families who were affected by the tragedy. Coming together in that broken moment in the middle of the afternoon was perhaps the most intimate moment I had in my seventeen years at ESPN.

After we finished, I said to Charlie, "I didn't know you were a praying man."

"Yeah," he said. "I grew up in the church, and I just knew you were deep in your faith, and I thought it was important to pray today. I knew I could come to you."

Though it was a painful day, that was a special moment. We came together in that room, united around suffering, just as the people of Boston came together that day. Those are the kinds of moments we'll all remember whenever we look back on our careers. Not our awards or successes or accolades but the fragile moments of life when we unite around suffering with our coworkers. When we come together as friends, as prayer warriors, as family, as companions who have one another's backs. A lot of people are afraid of this kind of deep connection in the workplace, but I believe it's what life is all about.

True impact—on a deep level, a heart level, a soul level—can't be measured or gauged the same as podcast downloads or social media statistics. Leaders, like the farmer in the parable, must invest in the day-to-day process—the tiny things happening behind the scenes that no one else is aware of—in order to stay the course and trust the process even when nothing about it can be measured.

THIS LIFE OF LEARNING TRUE LEADERSHIP IS A PROCESS, NOT A MICROWAVABLE MEAL.

This life of learning true leadership is a process, not a microwavable meal. Most days in the workplace are, after all, generally the same. They all run together. It's up to you as a leader to go, like the farmer in the parable, out into your own field hour after hour, day after day, with intention and diligence. Sticking to the process can lead to seeds being planted each day and beautiful mysteries unfolding beneath the surface.

Hebrews 12:1–2 exhorts us to "run with perseverance the race marked out for us, fixing our eyes on Jesus, the pioneer and perfecter of faith." You run the course that is uniquely yours, persevere with each step, focus on the prize, and allow yourself to be transformed in the process. We get so hung up on results—what we can or can't measure, can or can't see. But your job as a leader is simply to run with excellence.

I'm not saying I left a unique mark on Charlie, or on any of my coworkers, for that matter. I was just happy I was approachable at a time when he wanted to pray, on a broken day and in a vulnerable moment. I was happy he knew someone who would understand. Because of how I lived my life and what I stood for, he knew he could knock on my door. I was reminded that day that there were things happening beneath the surface in my relationships with people at work that simply could not be measured. At a really trying time, Charlie knew I was approachable. As the parable says, "Night and day, whether [the farmer] sleeps or gets up, the seed sprouts and grows, though he does not know how" (Mark 4:27).

PUTTING ON THE UNIFORM

Leading the right way does not always produce immediate results. It might not turn your season around immediately. It might not lead to profits or sales. It might not lead to deep conversations with coworkers. Your boss might not appreciate your efforts. You might not see a turnaround in your spouse or your kids today or tomorrow.

But if you put on the uniform of leadership consistently—if you bloom right where you're planted—you may have an influence you're unaware of. An effect that's unseen and that can't be measured because it happens beneath the surface. Call it culture. Call it impact. Call it meaning.

Go out into the field each day. Make other people your priority, and wait with active patience for what will happen. Just because you cannot see anything changing does not mean that something beautiful is not taking place. So keep putting on your uniform. Keep blooming. And trust your efforts. Results and measurements can be helpful in gauging whether certain strategies are working, but quarterly profits, victories, and sales do not gauge whether a culture is healthy or inspiring. And they're no indication of what might be happening beneath the surface.

DISCUSSING THE UNIFORM

▷ Think about the best coach or boss you ever had. What made that person so impactful in your life? Was their impact something measurable in your life, or was it beneath the surface, something meaningful they stirred within you? Explain.

▷ Why is it so difficult to trust your labor when you cannot see its fruit? What does this say about us and our culture?

▷ Sometimes our idea of the harvest is too worldly and performance-focused. How can you reframe the concept of "harvest" to focus on life's most important things? (For example, instead of obsessing over something you're trying to accomplish at work, what if you were to savor the meaningful time you spend with your family, a loving harvest that rises out of a gift God has given you?)

▷ What stands out to you, personally, about Jesus's parable of the growing seed?

8

FULL-TIME EXCELLENCE

THERE'S AN ADDED ASPECT TO the farmer in the parable in Mark 4. Not only must he be incredibly patient because the seeds he's planted take time to produce a harvest, but he also has to continually reinvest himself in the process. When the crop does come up and the harvest is reaped, it isn't long until the process starts all over again and the farmer goes right back to square one.

The best leaders invest themselves in processes rather than destinations. If they reach their desired destination, it's usually because they got absorbed in the journey.

No athlete I saw epitomized this more than New Orleans Saints quarterback Drew Brees. Drew came to ESPN on the longest day I have ever worked. It was at the beginning of July 2010, only about a month before Tony Dungy came to Bristol and posed the question that changed my life.

This particular day was absolute havoc. Not only was Drew, the reigning Super Bowl champion and Super Bowl MVP, coming to ESPN to promote his book *Coming Back Stronger*, but LeBron James would be making "The Decision" later that evening. On a program that would appear exclusively on ESPN, he would announce whether he would remain with the Cleveland Cavaliers or go elsewhere.

So we, the sports media, had not just one but two huge responsibilities. We were covering perhaps the biggest free agency news in NBA history. *And* we were hosting a quarterback who was on top of the sports world, having brought New Orleans their first (and only) Super Bowl championship, uniting a devastated city still rebuilding in the aftermath of Hurricane Katrina.

What made all this especially challenging was that two of our four talent producers—half of us—were on vacation. This left only me and my colleague Jamila to handle the chaos of the day. Our boss actually considered canceling the Car Wash with Drew Brees because of the lack of available talent producers and the pressures of the day following LeBron's decision. But we assured her we could handle it. How could we reschedule with the reigning Super Bowl MVP?

When I met Drew Brees early that morning, he was accompanied by his agent and the same publicist, Todd, who would join Coach Dungy a month later. After brief introductions, Todd mentioned something that caught me off guard: "Drew needs two hours to work out this afternoon. Could he do it in between shows?"

I thought about it, then said, "That shouldn't be a problem. ESPN has a nice gym on campus. What kind of workout does Drew want to do?"

"I think he just wants to get some cardio in," Todd responded, "but be prepared for anything else."

"Okay." I laughed, unsure what "anything else" could possibly mean.

The day began with Drew appearing on *Mike & Mike* and then on *First Take*. While spending time with him between shows, I noticed how cordial Drew was with everyone we interacted with. He seemed to enjoy promoting his book, which dove deep into several areas of his life—the adversity he faced and the faith he found—but he was also enjoying the day as a sports fan. He kept asking different people whether they thought LeBron was going to stay with the Cavs.

But the big lesson I learned from Drew came later in the morning, around eleven o'clock, when it came time for him to do his workout. In my time as a talent producer, I had worked with hundreds of athletes who exercise each day, but Drew was the first who was determined to get in his workout while at ESPN in the middle of the Car Wash. The others, I assumed, worked out in the evening after they had completed the Car Wash and returned home, or perhaps they took the day off. With Drew, however, it was apparent that he was on a regimented workout plan.

So I led Drew to the gym, and for about an hour, he ran on the treadmill and did other cardio-related exercises. Once he was finished, Drew asked me, "Is there a place I can throw some footballs?"

"What do you mean?" I asked, unsure what exactly he was looking to do.

"I just need some space to complete my drills," he replied.

I thought to myself, *Oh, gosh, where on campus is there space for Drew Brees to throw footballs?* Then I remembered the miniature football field right outside the cafeteria. ESPN had it professionally painted, with yard markers going up to about forty yards and an ESPN logo in the end zone. But the field was designed more for aesthetics, not as a training ground for a reigning Super Bowl MVP. Nor was the field private; it was right in front of the cafeteria, and we'd be using it right around the time ESPN employees were going to lunch.

I asked Drew anyway if the field would suffice and warned him there would be a lot of lunchtime traffic.

"Are you worried about people bothering you?" I asked.

"Not really," Drew said, "but I'd rather just be throwing to my agent, not anyone else."

"All right, we can do that," I said. "I'll get a security guy to monitor the field, and I'll also make sure that no one bothers you."

I guided Drew to the field while his agent fetched a football from his car. That was another first for me: an ESPN guest bringing his own athletic equipment to campus. I said to Drew, "I've never had a guest work out and train in the middle of the Car Wash before."

I think Drew understood I was trying to get him to explain why he worked out so intently and intensely. After all, he had just won the Super Bowl. Why not take a break? Drew said, "Somebody else is trying to take my job. If I don't do this, I'm giving that person who might be there today working out a chance to take my job."

For the next thirty to forty minutes, I watched a master craftsman improve as a quarterback right outside the ESPN cafeteria in the middle of a hot July afternoon in Bristol, Connecticut. He simulated short screen passes and thirty-yard down-the-field passes. He spun off of invisible pass rushers.

As the lunch crowd came and went, I noticed Drew was attracting a lot of attention and odd looks. I imagined people's thoughts: *Who is this short guy throwing footballs, thinking he is Drew Brees? Oh wait—it is Drew Brees!* The sidelines started brimming with onlookers watching the best quarterback in the world simulate passes right in front of them during their lunch break.

In the world's eyes, Drew Brees had made it to the mountaintop, having just won a Super Bowl, earning MVP honors, and helping to reconstruct a broken city. But to Drew Brees, there was someone behind him who wanted to take his job. There were many more improvements to his game that he could make. So many more games and championships he wanted to win for a city he loved. There was so much further he wanted to go, so much more of a career left to be played.

Training camp hadn't even begun yet. I'm sure many NFL players and coaches were still on vacation. But there was Drew Brees, on a day that was about promoting his book, determined to stay focused on perfecting his craft. It was about pursuing excellence with all his might, intention, and commitment. It was about dedication, diligence, discipline, and desire. It was about cultivating effort.

▼ ▼ ▼

Many in our society experience an emptiness when they finally get the thing they worked so hard to attain—a big home, a nice car, a well-paying job, the American Dream. All along, they were focusing on the wrong thing. Countless people's lives are dictated by trying to grab hold of something the world has elevated, not what they have personally decided was important. So many are living out of the cravings of their ego, not the deep parts of their soul.

I love what Colossians 3:17 says because it flips the world on its head: "Whatever you do, whether in word or deed, do it all in the name of the Lord Jesus, giving thanks to God the Father through him."

Life is about more than recklessly trying to accumulate things that the world says are important. Drew Brees understood that reaching his goal the year before didn't mean that pursuing excellence daily could take a back seat. He still had a job to do. That day at ESPN, he displayed very clearly that he was elevating something different than what the world was elevating. He was playing a different game than what the world was playing. And it came from a deep, true place within him.

When Todd first mentioned to me that Drew needed to work out, my knee-jerk thought was, *C'mon, Drew can take* one *day off.* But in Drew's mind, just because he'd won a Super Bowl didn't mean there weren't two guys behind him who wanted his starting position. Today as I write this, nine years later in 2019, it's obvious that his hard work and daily commitment to excellence have paid off. He was thirty-one years old then; he is forty years old now, still playing in the NFL, and he became the NFL all-time leader in passing yards in the 2018 season. But he realized that all he could do each day was focus on the current process.

The only things we can control in the process are our attitude and effort. Attitude is how we react to situations and invest in others through servant leadership. Effort is how we pursue excellence each moment and invest ourselves fully in the task at hand. The last chapter focused on the first concern: how to refine our attitude with a thermostat mentality. In this chapter, we'll zoom in on effort.

GOOD LEADERS ARE CONSTANTLY COMMITTING TO AND REFINING THEIR EFFORTS ON A DAILY BASIS.

Good leaders are constantly committing to and refining their efforts on a daily basis. The day Drew Brees came to ESPN—the day when the depth of his attitude and effort was on full display—also happened to be my longest workday in my seventeen years at ESPN. I didn't leave the office until after midnight. I couldn't control that half our talent producers were gone, that LeBron made a decision that rocked the sports world, or that Drew Brees came to ESPN on the day he did. All I could do was focus in on my own effort—my personal pursuit of excellence.

This truth has resurfaced in my life again and again. I've always had to work hard for anything in life. I didn't have the most stable childhood; it was riddled with verbal abuse by my alcoholic father, and early on I had to intentionally decide who I wanted to be and how I wanted to live. Though I wasn't a Christian yet, the trauma I experienced in my childhood shaped my decision to become a man of character and integrity. I committed to working hard and staying focused in life.

On a more practical level, I also had to invest myself fully in the classroom and in the arena of sports. While my brother was a valedictorian and star quarterback, I wasn't blessed with those same genes. I had to work my butt off just to get by in my classes and play a minimal role in athletics. What came naturally to me in the classroom, how high I jumped or how fast I was on the basketball court—those weren't things I could control. What I could control was my effort. And that was really all that mattered.

Drew Brees understands that he can't control whether his receiver drops a pass. He can't control how the New Orleans Saints defense plays. He can't control whether the officials make the right calls. But in each moment—throughout every practice session and in every game—he understands that he can control how he gives his energy to the situation. He is fully in charge of his own effort.

Whenever I lose focus on my purpose or concentrate too much on what the world deems important, I think about that day with Drew Brees. I think about my coworkers gathering around that miniature football field and witnessing a man of high character and unrelenting effort teaching us how to live by never ceasing to give his utmost, even though he was already on top of the world.

PUTTING ON THE UNIFORM

It's natural for us to want to control everything we possibly can in our world and in our lives. There's a lot that lies outside our power. But the parable of the growing seed reminds us that we *can* control our effort. When you put on the uniform today, set aside the urge to control what happens with the seed you plant and focus your effort instead on your personal pursuit of excellence. Replace your anxiety over things you can't control with a passion and conviction for the things you can. Transition from a results-rooted paradigm to an excellence-rooted paradigm. As Drew Brees exemplified that day, even at the top of the sports world, excellence has no bounds. It keeps expanding.

DISCUSSING THE UNIFORM

▷ What is inspiring to you about Drew Brees's attitude and effort? How does this story translate into your own world and what you are up against?

▷ What steps can you take mentally and emotionally to transition from being results-focused to excellence-focused? What are the differences between these two paradigms in your own world?

▷ How can you refine your attitude (how you react to situations) and your effort (how you pursue excellence and invest yourself in each moment) today? What are some of your blind spots?

9

WHERE IT ALL FLOWS FROM

I HAVE A FEELING ONE of the reasons Drew Brees works as hard as he does is because he's grateful for the skills and gifts he's been given, the city he loves, the family he serves, and the platform he has. I know there are hard workers out there who aren't thankful at all, people who are just focused on getting their hands on the next thing. But that kind of motivation is always fleeting. You eventually realize what I realized when I got my dismal midyear review—that the job I was working so hard to get didn't fulfill me the way I thought it would. It was just another job, just another title, perhaps better pay. The things in our lives that we turn into idols always seem to leave us feeling somewhat empty when we get them. Gratitude, on the other hand, is an animating force that produces a long-term work ethic and effort, a continual reinvestment in the process.

One of the best centering practices for wearing your uniform the right way every day is to adopt a posture of gratitude for where you are. Gratitude roots you in the present. Though our minds seem to cling to uncertainty or looking for the next thing to achieve, being thankful for where you are and what you get to do today opens your eyes to the blessings all around you. As the apostle Paul wrote in the book of Philippians, "Finally, brothers and sisters, whatever is true, whatever is noble, whatever is right, whatever is pure, whatever is lovely, whatever is admirable—if anything is excellent or praiseworthy—*think* about such things" (4:8, emphasis mine).

AN ATTITUDE OF GRATITUDE SETS THE TEMPERATURE IN YOUR ENVIRONMENT, INSPIRING THOSE YOU ARE LEADING THROUGH LOVE AND JOY RATHER THAN FEAR.

Intentionally dwelling on the many blessings in our lives, the revelations of God's love and grace, can help us reconfigure our minds, which are so prone to negativity and uncertainty. This is what makes an attitude of gratitude so empowering. It naturally overflows to other people and instills value in them. An attitude of gratitude sets the temperature in your environment, inspiring those you are leading through love and joy rather than fear.

In Jon Gordon's *The Carpenter*, Michael, whom the carpenter is mentoring, expresses frustration to the carpenter about only picking up a single customer one week when his company needed many more customers in order to keep up with their bills. The carpenter responds, "I see it differently. . . . I believe you should be thankful that you got a new customer. The more you are thankful, the more you will have things to be thankful for. The more you and your company appreciate each new client, the more you will become a magnet for new clients. This appears to be a wonderful growth opportunity for you and your company."[6]

In September 2012, we had a guest on the Car Wash who demonstrated a profound sense of gratitude. The guest was one of the most popular drivers in racing, Dale Earnhardt Jr. He was at ESPN the week before the "Chase for the Championship," NASCAR's version of the postseason. However, his visit came right at the start of the NFL season, and it didn't take me long to see Dale Jr.'s love for the NFL and Fantasy Football.

I didn't tell Dale, a die-hard Washington Redskins fan, that I myself was a Dallas Cowboys loyalist because, well, I wanted the day to go well. I wanted him to like me. What I did do was arrange for us to grab lunch with Fantasy Football expert Matthew Berry. It was my job as a talent producer to make sure each guest at ESPN had as enjoyable an experience as possible. This entailed feeling out their different passions and sports interests and doing whatever I could to connect them with people within the intricate network at ESPN whom they would enjoy getting to know. It was the least we could to for our Car Wash guests who were spending the entire day with us, hopping from show to show, expending their energy and sacrificing their time.

Dale Jr. loved eating lunch with Matthew Berry and drilled him with questions about Fantasy Football. He really must've wanted to beat the tar out of whoever was in his fantasy league, because Dale's questions for Matthew were unending.

Later that afternoon, after I had left work to pick up my daughter from school, I received a text while I was waiting in the school parking lot. I didn't recognize the number. It was Dale Jr., thanking me for spending my day with him and for my hospitality. He even suggested we keep in touch.

Never as a talent producer had I received a text directly from a guest after our day together. And it's not like we had exchanged numbers either. He must have gotten mine from someone and taken the time to text me a personal thank-you.

He didn't need to do that. After all, I was just doing my job. I was getting paid by ESPN to take care of its Car Wash guests and make their experience a pleasant one. But Dale Jr. still took the time to thank me directly. His simple gratitude spilled over to me and made such an impression that I remember it clearly seven years later.

Taking time to extend such a personal touch moves people deeply. It makes them feel appreciated and valued.

It's common in our world to hear "Well, that's their job," or "That's what they're getting paid to do," as if that warrants treating others thanklessly for their work. This attitude is especially prevalent in the corporate world. Rarely do people thank workers at the lowest level of the company's operation. The janitors. The cafeteria workers. The interns. Lots of bosses and executives don't thank their employees because, in their minds, they are paying their employees to work, so why thank them.

Gratitude, however, is contagious. It spreads like wildfire. When people feel valued for what they do, they will go on to thank others and instill value in them. Employees and teammates who feel valued are going to work that much harder for their bosses and coaches.

▼ ▼ ▼

Gratitude holds everything together and is the glue that connects us all to one another. But unique displays of gratitude, like the text that Dale Jr. sent me, are often lacking in a world of people who are predominantly selfish, focused on what they can get rather than what they can give. Personal touches of thanks and affirmation remind us of our connectedness to one another. In the workplace, gratitude unites us around the processes that are being put into motion. And at home and in our personal lives, it brings us together around the love and grace in life that are to be experienced and enjoyed.

This is one reason why I send my daughter a text message every morning. Sometimes the texts are deep or spiritual. Other times they are just uplifting, like "You're awesome! I'm so proud of you!"

No matter what I send her, my goal is for it always to be encouraging and affirming. And yes, not even her missing the bus can prevent my texts from coming to her each morning.

Maybe these texts don't mean much to her now, or maybe they do. Maybe in her teenage years they feel like just another silly thing her corny father does in his parenting. Or maybe some days the texts are exactly what she needs to hear. I don't really care what she thinks of them, because I'm sure that one day she'll do the same thing for her own child or with her own friends. Most people who tear others down never felt valued themselves and struggle with their own self-worth; I want my daughter to know she is deeply loved in the Romano family. Her value doesn't depend on whether she's having a good day or a bad day. Whether she's getting straight As or struggling in her academics. Whether she had a good softball game the night before or struck out each time at bat. Her performance doesn't matter. She belongs.

The personal touch we show others flows out of our gratitude for them.

I wish bosses and coaches could understand just how far a personal touch of gratitude can go. I once received handwritten thank-you notes from both Clemson University's head football coach, Dabo Swinney, and University of Virginia's head basketball coach, Tony Bennett, after having them on our *Sports Spectrum Podcast*. I was pleasantly shocked. Their teams were topmost in their leagues at the time, yet these men took the time and thought to write me. That said a lot about how hands-on and personal they are as leaders.

Such gestures don't have to be anything big. They can be small, almost effortless displays of how much people around us matter. If my daughter's softball coaches ever pulled her to the side when she was struggling or in a slump and simply said, "Stay at it. You matter to this team and have a unique role to play, whether you go 0-for-4 or 4-for-4," their words would empower her and give her confidence in unfathomable ways. They would also help her see beyond her personal performance and consider her role on the team—the unique gifts she has to offer through her leadership and personality. This is the only way a healthy and inspiring culture can be constructed: for a bond to form among group members that goes far beyond winning and achieving.

To tell someone you appreciate them, to let a person know they are a vital cog in the machine—these little personal touches go far. Some of the most underappreciated players in sports are the fullback in football and relief pitcher or backup catcher in baseball. But so many athletes who came through ESPN and Sports Spectrum have told me that the most valuable player on their team is its fullback, relief pitcher, or backup catcher. The most successful team cultures are the ones that acknowledge those players and elevate them just as much as the Tom Bradys and Mike Trouts.

A clip in the 2019 NCAA tournament that went viral shows former Virginia Tech head coach Buzz Williams praying with his three seniors on the bench after the team lost and was eliminated from the tourney. It wasn't a hyperspiritual prayer. It was essentially, "God, thank you for Joe. He is an amazing person. He wants to make people better. Joe is going to do great things for this world because he loves people. We are so grateful Joe is here."

Whether or not you're a spiritual person, and no matter how you feel about prayer, you can't tell me this display of affection from a head coach didn't instill value in those three players outside their performance and let them know how much they meant to him and the team. That's the heart of Jesus. In the New Testament, we continually see Jesus meeting people where they are—particularly those on the outside of religion—and loving them just for themselves. Similarly, Coach Williams cared enough about each of those young athletes, regardless of whether they were star players, to express how he felt about them in front of the whole team and, it turns out, the entire country. I have a feeling those three men will remember that moment the rest of their lives and try to help others feel the way their head coach made them feel as college basketball players.

BE AWARE NOT ONLY OF OTHERS' EFFORTS BUT ALSO OF THE KIND OF ENERGY YOU'RE GIVING TOWARD SITUATIONS.

Be like Coach Williams and Dale Jr. Go the extra mile to show others gratitude. Be aware not only of others' efforts but also of the kind of energy you're giving toward situations.

A friend of mine is a manager. He carries five pennies in his left pocket, and every time he says "thank you" or something nice to an employee, he moves one penny to his right pocket. Every time he has to correct someone, he moves two pennies back to his left pocket. His goal every day is to leave with all the pennies in his right pocket. If you can find a way to cultivate this kind of awareness throughout the day about how grateful you are for others and their efforts, you'll begin to be viewed as an encouraging leader. Your culture will become more positive and inspiring.

PUTTING ON THE UNIFORM

Most of us tend to focus on what we don't have or how we're not where we want to be in life. Our brains seem to naturally cling to unknowing, difficulty, or anything in life that lacks resolve. It takes intentionality to focus on what we are thankful for in life and cultivate an attitude of gratitude.

Begin developing a discipline of gratitude that works for you. Maybe whenever you eat a meal, thank God for something that happened in your day. Or start a gratitude journal, listing ten things you're grateful for every night before you go to bed.

As you develop a discipline that is best for you, you'll find yourself enjoying life more and savoring more of your moments. And your attitude will ultimately spill over onto others. You'll naturally affirm people and see their strengths rather than judging them and focusing on their flaws.

Athletes will struggle to enjoy the game at hand if they focus on the mistakes of the past, whether their own or their teammates'. Be known as a leader who enjoys the game, savors the moments, and thanks those he or she has been entrusted to lead. Gratitude is the antidote to people's lack of presence. It will open your eyes to the beauty of life and inspire you to instill value in others.

DISCUSSING THE UNIFORM

▷ Identify a place or two in your life where unknowing, difficulty, or a lack of resolve is eating up your mental or emotional energy. What would it look like to develop an attitude of gratitude in the tension?

▷ Spend the next five minutes praying a prayer of thanks. Don't ask for anything. Don't focus on what is lacking. Simply identify what is good. How do you feel after the exercise? What did you learn from this exercise?

▷ Loving and affirming others begins with loving and affirming your own life that God has given you. What are you thankful for in your life? What are you grateful for regarding your own talents, skills, gifts, and passions? Write down the things you are thankful for.

▷ When it comes to those you have been entrusted to lead, whom can you do a better job of loving and affirming? How do you plan to do that? What are some practical steps you can take to show them how valued they are?

10

THE TRUE MEANING OF PLATFORM

WHEN YOU'RE THANKFUL TO BE where you are each day, daring to find the blessings in the challenges, you may find yourself being more outward-focused than inward-focused. You may be more aware of the needs of others. You might use whatever platform you have to help others and brighten their day, just like Tami always did. Each of us has been given a sphere of influence, but it's your choice whether you view your platform as something that lifts *you* up or as something you can use to lift up others.

When you take the time to validate others' efforts, as Dale Jr. did for me through his thank-you text, you may find yourself also creating special moments for people—moments that become memories. It's important for a leader to become increasingly outward-focused over time in order to leave lasting, positive imprints on others.

Back in 2007, seven years into working at ESPN, I was still entranced by the environment at the network's Bristol campus. All around me were broadcasters I had listened to throughout high school and college and anchors I watched daily on television. Every day there were athletes visiting campus, many of whom were god-like figures to me. Some people don't understand how others can be so obsessed with sports, and that's okay, but for me, sports has been as integral to my life as the air I breathe.

Sports helped me to cope with the struggles and the traumas of my childhood. When I was hiding from my dad or trying to forget about his drunken fits of rage, sports was where I found solace. I still have my piles of notebooks filled with handwritten Boston Celtics stats, diligently documented as I watched my favorite basketball player, Larry Bird, dominate the hardwood. I still have boxes of my old baseball cards, including a whole stack of cherished Darryl Strawberry and Doc Gooden cards, two New York Mets greats whom I worshiped as a kid. When it comes to sports, I have a photographic memory; to this day, I could probably recite stats, dates, and specifics about a particular season for any of my favorite professional teams, whether it's the Celtics, the Mets, or the Dallas Cowboys.

As I grew older and my situation with my alcoholic father worsened, sports remained my escape, a place I belonged and could call home, even if it was just me with a notebook watching the Celtics alone in my bedroom and keeping stats. I know—I'm a nerd.

ESPN never lost its luster for me, but I definitely settled in over time and became less starstruck by the athletes I got to meet and work beside. I realized they were just people like me. Back in 2007, however, I wasn't working so frequently with athletes face-to-face; I spent most of my time on the telephone and computer, booking guests for *OTL*.

One day I heard through the grapevine that Hall of Fame Cowboys running back Emmitt Smith would be visiting ESPN. Now, anyone who knew me well in the nineties knows that Emmitt was my guy. I had his jersey. I kept scrapbooks of his stats. I had posters of him hung up in my dorm room. It was a formative time of my life when I was, for the first time, creating boundaries between my father and me, making decisions about my future, taking ownership of my life, and becoming more empowered in who I wanted to become. The joy Emmitt brought me in those days, watching him on the gridiron, is to this day difficult for me to put into words. Even when I married my wife, Dawn, I think she knew Emmitt would come first in my life until he retired. (Just kidding . . . I think. Dawn and I have been happily married since his retirement.)

Anyway . . . ESPN is a massive campus, but it still shocked me that Emmitt and I would be in the same vicinity and I might even cross paths with him, maybe see him in the hallways.

About an hour before Emmitt got to campus, I received an email from *NFL LIVE* host Trey Wingo. It had six simple words: "Do you want to meet Emmitt?"

Uhhh . . .

"I would really enjoy that," I responded, trying to sound casual.

He fired back: "Okay, meet me in the newsroom at two o'clock."

I didn't care what I was supposed to be doing at two o'clock. I didn't even check my schedule to see if I had a meeting. All I knew was that I was going to be in the newsroom.

That afternoon, excited out of my mind and needing to talk about it, I gave my wife a call.

"Dawn, I'm about to meet Emmitt Smith," I said.

She paused and replied, "Are you okay?"

"No," I said bluntly.

If my heart exploded in my chest, she would at least know what happened. In all seriousness, I had no idea how I was going to handle it. It was a *really* big deal for me. If you've ever met one of your childhood heroes, perhaps you understand.

At a quarter till two, I went over to the newsroom Trey had directed me to. Trey shook my hand and told me he would introduce me to Emmitt when the time was right. And that's when I saw Emmitt come into the studio. I watched him interact with people in the newsroom. I was in awe that I was in the same room with him,

standing on the same floor as the feet of perhaps the greatest running back of all time. This was holy ground.

I hung out in the background as he got acclimated and Trey
guided him around the studio. I tried to act casual, hoping no one
there could see the sweat on my nose and forehead. Trey then told
me to follow them over to Studio E, where he would film a segment
with Emmitt for *NFL Live*. I walked through the ESPN halls, trail-
ing Trey and Emmitt and a small group Emmitt had brought with
him that day, and into Studio E.

That was when Trey said, "Emmitt, I wanted to introduce you
to someone. This is Jason Romano, one of our producers here. He's
a really good guy. I'm going to get ready for the segment, and I'll be
back in a few minutes." Trey was giving me five minutes alone with
my childhood sports hero!

I don't even remember what Emmitt and I talked about. Thank-
fully, I wasn't like Chris Farley in the hilarious *Saturday Night Live*
sketch with Paul McCartney where Chris, playing a nervous television host, asks Paul, "Remember when you were with the Beatles?"
But I might have been close. The fact I can't remember anything
(and trust me, I remember *everything*) is without doubt a reflection
on how nervous I really was. I think Emmitt and I talked about his
retirement and how he won *Dancing with the Stars* or something. I
don't know.

Before it was time for Emmitt to film his segment, I asked his
agent if he would take a picture of us. I had brought my digital camera with me (remember those days?). Four years later, when I met
Emmitt a second time, I got him to sign the picture. Maybe he was
just being nice, but he said he remembered me.

What Trey did for me always stuck with me. He went completely out of his way to make somebody else's day. He didn't have
to do it and he didn't gain anything from it. But a lot of people at
ESPN knew how much I loved Emmitt, and Trey had the awareness

to help a young producer kid have a chance to meet his hero. Not only that, but he strategically set it up so I could have time alone, face-to-face, with Emmitt. It meant the world to me.

▼ ▼ ▼

Business and athletics are cutthroat industries. People step on each other for advancement. They backstab one another to gain favor with superiors. It's often all about the individual rather than the collective, personal ambition rather than the team. People's souls get lost in hierarchy. Genuine relationships between two people are difficult to find because it's all about moving upward in the world.

But Trey that day viewed Emmitt's coming to ESPN as a selfless opportunity to serve. I was a nobody, just a booker. There wasn't a lot I could do for Trey at that point in my career, but he still went out of his way to make my day. A lot of good deeds have an underlying motive, but Trey had no agenda. No "you owe me" card he was trying to play. In a culture that is all about transaction and quid pro quo, Trey just wanted to be kind and use his platform to lift others up. And that is part of what made him a great leader.

The book of 2 Samuel gives a beautiful account in the ninth chapter of an interaction between King David and a man named Mephibosheth, the son of David's late, dear friend Jonathan. Mephibosheth's legs had been wounded when he was a baby, when his nurse took him and fled the city after his father and grandfather, Saul, died in battle. Perhaps she had dropped Mephibosheth in her panic. In any case, he had been unable to walk ever since. And as in our culture, people with physical defects in that day were often discriminated against, judged to be under God's wrath because of their sin. Mephibosheth's name, in fact, meant "mouth of shame." It is likely poor Mephibosheth had been forgotten by society and taken advantage of because of his condition.

In this touching scene, however, David, with all his power and influence, summoned Mephibosheth and told him, "'Don't be afraid, . . . for I will surely show you kindness for the sake of your father Jonathan. I will restore to you all the land that belonged to your grandfather Saul, and you will always eat at my table'" (2 Samuel 9:7). David had the authority to reinstate Mephibosheth's inheritance, and he had the awareness and conviction to do it. Good leaders are not afraid to do the right thing, even if it means going against the cultural narrative or out of their way to make something happen. They validate people's worth by creating special moments for them. They do all they can, given their unique influence, to empower others.

As my experience at ESPN allowed me to work different positions over the next decade, I eventually began working with athletes and celebrities daily as a talent producer. In that role, I followed Trey's example and did everything I could to connect people with their heroes, whether it was arranging for my mentor's son to meet Dwayne "The Rock" Johnson or for two of my coworkers to eat lunch with Darryl Strawberry. If I knew that a guest under my care at ESPN had a deep impact on a fellow employee or a friend, I always did my best to connect them for five minutes if possible. Given a little more influence at ESPN and the freedom to make things happen, I loved doing for others what Trey had done for me.

AS LEADERS, WE HAVE THE OPPORTUNITY TO MAKE A BIG IMPACT ON OTHER PEOPLE WITHOUT LOOKING FOR REPAYMENT.

As leaders, we have the opportunity to make a big impact on other people without looking for repayment. Think about it. If every one of us gave to others the way the most generous people have given to us, there would be an overflow of love and grace to help heal the broken leadership model in our culture. It doesn't have to involve as impressive a deed as reinstating someone's societal standing and delivering an inheritance, as King David did for Mephibosheth, or as magnanimous as helping someone meet their childhood hero, as Trey Wingo did for me. Creating a special moment for another person could entail taking someone who's having a hard time out to lunch or helping a fellow employee pay one of their bills during a period of financial distress. It could involve connecting a person with someone who can help them put their dreams in motion or otherwise supporting that person in his or her pursuits. The question for you to ask as a leader is, How can I use the gifts, resources, influence, or abundance God has given me to make a special moment for someone else?

PUTTING ON THE UNIFORM

Our world is transactional in nature. People feel the pressure of playing their cards right so they can climb higher in the world and get the raise, the house, the prestige, the American Dream, the influence, the reputation. It seems that everyone is trying to build their own platform in some way. This desire for upward movement and building up one's domain often results in hidden agendas and a give-to-get approach to relationships. When life is all about you, that's all life can be. But it isn't good leadership. The ego boosts feel good briefly. The material possessions are enticing for a time. But everyone with this disposition ultimately finds themselves at a dead end, forced to confront their emptiness and despair.

The true meaning of platform—of success—is using whatever skills, gifts, influence, and material possessions you have to lift up others, not yourself. If you're not helping others be successful—if you're not helping others to create special moments in life—then you're missing the point. Your life is not your own. It must flow out of a source of love onto others.

DISCUSSING THE UNIFORM

▷ What does success mean to you? What has it meant to you in the past? What life experiences have helped you refine your definition of success?

▷ Think about a time when someone used their platform or resources to lift you up and help you experience a special moment. How did this make you feel? What was the lasting impact?

▷ How can you use the skills, gifts, influence, and resources you've been given to be a blessing to others?

▷ Reflect on this quote from author Jon Gordon: "You aren't a true success unless you are helping others be successful. Success is meant to be shared."[7] Apply this to your life. What does it mean to you? How does it convict you, inspire you, or affirm you regarding the direction you're taking in life?

The first-ever ESPN Fellowship Group with Pro Football Hall of Fame coach Bobby Bowden in center, August 2014.

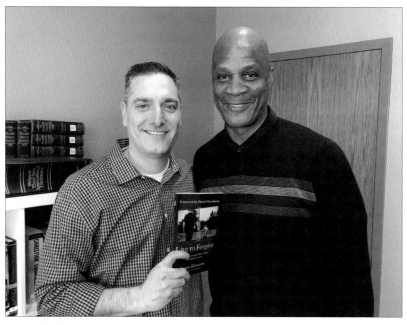

Jason with Darryl Strawberry at a men's conference in Wisconsin, January 2018.

Jason with Dwayne "The Rock" Johnson in the ESPN *SportsCenter* studio in Bristol, Connecticut, January 2012.

Jason speaking at a conference in Florida, December 2019.

Jason meets Dallas Cowboys Hall of Famer Emmitt Smith for the first time at ESPN, January 2007.

Jason with coach Tony Dungy and writer Nathan Whitaker at ESPN, August 2010.

Jason and former New England Patriots All-Pro tight end Rob Gronkowski, March 2013.

At Walt Disney World's Disney Springs in Orlando, Florida, with *Mike & Mike* crew, January 2017.

At the EA Sports Madden Cover Event in New York City with NFL running back Adrian Peterson and Detroit Lions Hall of Famer Barry Sanders, April 2013.

Jason with ESPN's Mike Greenberg, Mike Golic, and Chris Berman at the ESPN studios.

Jason at the ESPN studios with New Orleans Saints quarterback Drew Brees, August 2010.

Jason at the ESPN studios with Seattle Seahawks Super Bowl–winning coach Pete Carroll, July 2010.

Jason with *Mike & Mike* staff member Paul Hembekides in front of Wrigley Field in Chicago, October 2016.

Jason's final day at ESPN with *Mike & Mike*, February 10, 2017.

Jason at the 2016 NCAA Final Four at the NRG Stadium in Houston, Texas, April 2016.

11

THE ART OF AWARENESS

WHEN YOU'RE IN AN INFLUENTIAL position like Trey Wingo, you can make big things happen, like arranging for a young producer to meet one of the greatest running backs of all time. I never forgot what Trey did for me. It stuck with me moving forward.

But being a leader isn't just about grand actions or doing things that might one day end up as a story in a book. If someone has the power or the influence to make big splashes of impact, that's great. But the truth is that leadership is more about being aware of people's daily needs—being outward-focused—and doing the *little things* each day that let others know they are valued. Everyone carries a burden of some sort, whether personal or professional. Seeing those burdens and then daily doing little things to lighten them is a much truer reflection of a person's character and integrity than doing the things everyone talks about.

In the fall of 2009, one of the top college quarterbacks at the time, University of Texas's Colt McCoy, was visiting ESPN along with a number of his teammates and much of the Texas football staff. I was asked to meet them all in the cafeteria and facilitate breakfast before they reported to another studio. I was in the back of the cafeteria, picking up several gallons of milk to bring over to the team, when Colt walked up to me and asked how he could help. He could see I had my hands full. I gave him a gallon of milk and a case of donuts so I could carry something else.

It was a small gesture on Colt's part. Minimal—but also profound.

Colt had a whole entourage around him that day who were arguably there because of the success he was having that year. He was in the running for the Heisman Trophy. Texas was undefeated. They were ranked number two in the country. Colt was on top of the college football world. He was most certainly the king of Texas. Yet he did not see himself as someone to be served. He saw himself as a servant.

It was my job that day to serve them breakfast. That's what I was getting paid to do. I wasn't looking for help. I didn't need help. But Colt was aware enough to see that I, a complete stranger to him, had my hands full. He saw it as an opportunity to lend a helping hand. He was nowhere close to the football field, but his leadership was on full display. His desire to serve was on full display.

I believe that *awareness* is the key word here.

Like any good quarterback, Colt saw everything around him. But this wasn't just on the football field. Everywhere he went he saw opportunities to serve. The people around him he could help.

Good leaders cultivate two kinds of awareness. One is *self-awareness*: the ability to journey inward, to be aware of our thoughts and emotions, our tendencies, our insecurities, our ego. This inner awareness allows us to navigate the challenges of the day, recognize when we are off center, and adjust accordingly. Otherwise, how can we be a solid foundation for others when we ourselves are reactive or insecure? How can we be a thermostat in our outer environment if we're a thermometer in our inner world?

The second kind of awareness is *others awareness*: sensitivity to those around us and the situations they're in. Self-absorbed people are often blind to the needs of others. They fail to discern the opportunities to lend a helping hand because they are caught up in their own goals or problems. When people are struggling in life, feeling down or angry or frustrated, I always tell them, "Take yourself out of the picture and serve someone else."

A POSTURE OF SERVICE HAS A WAY OF FREEING US UP MENTALLY, EMOTIONALLY, AND SPIRITUALLY BECAUSE WE SHIFT OUR FOCUS FROM OUR OWN PROBLEMS TO OTHERS.

Much like forgiveness, a posture of service has a way of freeing us up mentally, emotionally, and spiritually because we shift our focus from our own problems to others. We are social beings, and we need one another; yet we seem to have forgotten this in our me-focused society. Most people go about their days focused on their own path, failing to see all the intersections with others along the way. What's your self-view? Someone who just wants to acquire or accomplish or accumulate things? Or someone who is here to humbly serve?

However you may feel about the person of Jesus, whether you believe he was the Messiah or whether you even believe in God, it would be hard to deny that Jesus was a good leader. He sparked a movement that changed the world. Though he was lifted up by others as a king, as the one who was the long-awaited Messiah, he had "no place to lay his head" (Luke 9:58) and proclaimed that he "did not come to be served, but to serve, and to give his life as a ransom for many" (Matthew 20:28). He did not use his influence to gain power or manipulate others or accumulate possessions, unlike many others later on who used his gospel for their own self-ish gain.

Whereas his disciples often got caught up in the hierarchical ways of the world and asked him which one of them was best, and whereas the Pharisees often got caught up in their hunger for power and frequently asked him who was right and who was wrong, Jesus deconstructed the manipulative ways of the world, lived simply and humbly, and said that the two greatest commandments were merely to love God and love others. The Jewish people at that time wanted him to be a conquering savior who would overthrow the Roman government, but instead he was born in a manger where the animals fed, rode a lowly donkey during his triumphal entry into Jerusalem, and was a suffering savior and servant.

In his letter to the Philippian believers, the apostle Paul shares a beautiful and inspiring discourse about Jesus's humility that is especially relevant for leaders today. Paul writes:

> Therefore if you have any encouragement from being united with Christ, if any comfort from his love, if any common sharing in the Spirit, if any tenderness and compassion, then make my joy complete by being like-minded, having the same love, being one in spirit and of one mind. Do nothing out of selfish ambition or vain conceit. Rather, in humility value others above yourselves, not looking to your own interests but each of you to the interests of the others.
>
> In your relationships with one another, have the same mindset as Christ Jesus:
>
> Who, being in very nature God,
>   did not consider equality with God something
> to be used to his own advantage;

> rather, he made himself nothing
>> by taking the very nature of a servant,
>> being made in human likeness.
> And being found in appearance as a man,
>> he humbled himself
>> by becoming obedient to death—
>>> even death on a cross!
>>>>> (Philippians 2:1–8)

It seems that everyone wants to be a king or queen these days—to be powerful, influential, successful. The world is about moving upward and emulating those higher up; so many people want to sit on the throne and bark orders downward. This, they think, is a demonstration of influence and power.

But Jesus, the greatest leader and revolutionary of all time, led with radical humility. His generosity was contagious, igniting a movement that was all about loving and serving others. For Jesus, nothing was below him. No one was outside his love. No task was a waste of his time. His humble posture allowed him to connect with anyone and to serve in the most unlikely places. Just because he preached and captivated thousands did not stop him from spending time with little children. He did not care about image. He did not care about status. He did not care about material possessions. He spent his time with people on the margins of society and hand-picked uneducated disciples to start his church. During his life, he dedicated himself to showing all in Galilee how deeply loved they were by God; in his death, he wore a crown of thorns and allowed himself to be crucified; and following his resurrection, he appeared first to women, who at that time had no social standing, and asked them to proclaim the wonderful news. His humility took him places no one else would go and inspired others to do the same—and it does so still today.

PUTTING ON THE UNIFORM

Our culture tends to link having an impact with making a massive splash in society; we connect it with the influence wielded by some of our favorite authors, athletes, pastors, or celebrities. But you don't have to have that kind of grand platform to make a difference. The size of your platform does not matter, nor is it up to you to control how big it is.

Focus on doing the little things each day. They could have a more powerful impact on those around you than any best-selling book or viral sermon ever could. When an athlete takes the field, his or her impact on the game, teammates, fans, and city must entail doing the little things. Sure, there might come a time when that player gets to make a diving catch, hit a walk-off home run, or even win a title. There might be an opportunity to host a big fundraiser or start a charity. But when it comes to the day-to-day, it's all about the player's awareness of the little things:

- The teammate who is going through some personal struggles and needs to be encouraged
- The kid in the stands wearing the player's jersey whose day would be made if he got to meet his hero
- The flight attendant with weary eyes who has had a long day and could use a smile or word of thanks

A person's *inner* awareness of where he or she is at mentally, emotionally, and spiritually, and the *outer* awareness of others and situations, is what makes someone a leader. It's what begets the small but vital actions throughout the day. Wearing the uniform of leadership, you realize that each week is less about the big moments and more about the hundreds of small ones every single day.

DISCUSSING THE UNIFORM

▷ Cultivating inner and outer awareness can be difficult because we often are stuck in our own heads, our own worlds, or the stories we tell ourselves, which are not always true. What steps can you take to cultivate an awareness that, throughout the day, will benefit your own health and enrich the days of others?

▷ Think of someone in your life who always seems to do the little things that help your day go more smoothly. What can you learn from that person's heart, spirit, and approach to life?

▷ What steps can you take to free yourself from a tunnel-vision or destination-focused approach to life and get back to the present?

12

A General's Culture

When you focus on doing the little things each day as an outward-focused, servant-hearted leader, a healthy culture will begin to form around you. Every leader longs to create good culture, but not everyone knows how. It takes consistency. It takes continually elevating others. It takes seeing them in their situation and meeting them where they are. Do the little things over time and you may have more than a positive impact—you just might create a lasting legacy. That's what happened with Bob Ley.

Nicknamed "The General"—partly because his name resembles Robert E. Lee but also because he was on the frontlines of ESPN's growth and popularity—Bob is one of the two on-air personalities who were with ESPN from the very beginning. (The other is Chris Berman). An iconic *SportsCenter* host who also founded ESPN's investigative television show *Outside the Lines*, Bob had arguably more credibility and influence than anyone else at ESPN, but it never got to his head. On top of being an incredible journalist and broadcaster, he was also the consummate leader and culture creator.

I first got connected with Bob in 2003. Desiring to transition from radio to the television world, I applied for a booker position at *Outside the Lines*. ESPN initially gave the position to someone they believed was more qualified, as I hadn't worked a day in television. Five months later, however, they reached back out to me, and I jumped on the opportunity immediately. What I didn't know then was that my time at *Outside the Lines* would change my career moving forward. It is still something I return to often in my mind for personal inspiration about leadership and culture.

When I first met Bob, I couldn't help but feel a little starstruck and awed. *Oh my goodness*, I thought. *This is The General. A legend. And I'm going to be working for* his *show.*

As excited as I was, I could also feel the pressure. I was anxious. I came in at a time right when *OTL* was transitioning from a weekly show to a daily show. This was one of the reasons they desperately needed a booker—because they needed guests for the show each day. But it was a hard show to book because it included a lot of controversial topics people didn't want to talk about on the air. If you were going on *OTL* with the hard-hitting journalist Bob Ley, you knew you had to know your stuff and be able to eloquently articulate your position. My job would be challenging. I embraced it.

Before I officially began, I wondered what the environment on Bob's staff would be like from day to day. After all, the show was already kind of an outlier. Under Bob's command, his staff had embarked on something no other show had dared to do. Most other shows were based on news, entertainment, or even personalities, but *OTL* was *investigative*, focused on in-depth reporting about serious topics. People who worked there were kind of viewed as the misfits at ESPN, off doing their own thing their own way. An eclectic group of six or seven people, the *OTL* staff had their own identity. And now I got to be a part of this offbeat group.

I wondered how Bob would act from day to day. He was one of the most powerful and tenured broadcasters at ESPN, after all. I had heard of some big hosts in the industry who were very distant from their staffs—who would hop in the studio to film their segment yet never build relationships with those who were putting the show together. I had heard stories about people who used their tenure and influence to be above reproach and make sure things were done *their* way. What I quickly learned, however, was that Bob was not only a talented journalist and reporter but also an expert culture creator. He was without a doubt a thermostat, and the one-of-a-kind culture he helped create was related to his collection of thermostat choices—week after week, month after month, year after year.

And he made sure he was available to help control the temperature in the room. He was hands-on in every way. He attended every staff meeting at eight o'clock in the morning (a lot of hosts in the industry wouldn't attend these meetings). And after the four o'clock show, when a lot of hosts get out of the studio as quickly as possible, there was Bob at the brief post-show meeting to reflect *with* us about what went well that day and what could be improved. Not only was Bob present, he was also submissive. He offered his opinions in these meetings, but he always let the producers call the shots. And whatever they decided, he fully committed to. He understood that no matter how long he had been at ESPN, his producers were the ones who were producing him, not the other way around. He was involved but was the exact opposite of micromanaging. He knew he didn't have all the answers.

I quickly saw that while I might have come to *Outside the Lines* thinking it was Bob's show, he certainly didn't see it that way. It was the staff's show. It was ESPN's show. It was anything but his.

No wonder a lot of people's brands, companies, and churches catastrophically implode: a single person's identity and ego gets too tied up in their direction. They become more about a dominant personality on camera or on the stage, more about a single person's ego than about the collective whole. So when that person falls, the whole group falls.

But not with Bob Ley. It was all about the team, even though he had been at ESPN almost longer than all of us combined. That's what struck me about Bob from the very start—how empowering he was to his team. It gave me confidence and boldness. It gave me the courage to try new things. Even when I made a suggestion that was off base, he validated me for my passion and hunger. And when I made a mistake, he challenged me to learn and grow and to improve the next time.

Two or three months into my time there, Bob looked me in the eyes and told me, "If you want to be a producer in this business, you have what it takes." Words cannot fully capture how much that meant to me—Bob Ley, a veteran and ESPN legend, saying those words to a guy working his first year in television. He didn't have to do that. He didn't have to go out of his way to tell me that. He'd had hundreds of producers over the years, people he had worked with and trusted, but he was aware enough and willing to invest in me. His encouragement propelled me forward. It showed me he believed in me. He took me under his wing.

I felt that Bob saw each of us at our depth for the gifts and skills we had to offer. It made sense. What good would a general be if he merely climbed the ranks but forgot about the real lives of those he was leading? Would his people feel moved to fight for him? For his cause? Would they be inspired to selfless deeds? We all knew that Bob, though uniquely leading us, was also fighting alongside us. He created space for our individual creativity and innovation and brilliance to unfold. He created space for us to flourish. And he had the respect of all of us. Like a good general, Bob was not shouting orders from safely behind castle walls. He was *in the fight* with his employees, journeying with us every step of the way, strengthening each of us and empowering us in our direction as we created something beautiful and meaningful together.

The precedent he set was even more important, considering the intensity of *OTL*. You knew you had to bring your A-game each day because of the seriousness and depth of the subjects we were covering. You knew you were working with a legend who, just as he believed in you, also wasn't afraid to push you. There were a few times each year when I saw Bob come down hard on people. But that's what the best leaders do. They strategically pick the times when they need to get the team re-centered or push individuals to the next level. But they do it in the context of belonging. The environment they create never becomes animated by fear but is instead rooted in excellence.

Bob had no ego whatsoever. There was no "Don't you know who I am?" attitude with him. He was one of us. He never asked people to cater to him. It was always about the team, the show, and the greater purpose of things: the investigative stories we were uncovering for the good of the public. He saw himself as playing a small part in the greater good.

What Bob's dedication to humble "with-ness" in our group ultimately did, in my opinion, was create a one-of-a-kind culture that had an unshakable identity and was always moving forward. We all felt we *belonged* on that special team. We felt safe in that culture, and our sense of security made us want to work as hard as we possibly could. Knowing Bob had our backs created a safe space for us to try things no other staff in sports media had tried before.

▼ ▼ ▼

I recently watched a TED Talk titled "Why Good Leaders Make You Feel Safe," delivered by management theorist Simon Sinek. He had a notepad on stage, and on it he wrote "DANGER" in every corner, then drew a circle in the center with the word "SAFE" inside. He told the audience:

> It's the leader that sets the tone. When a leader makes the choice to put the safety and lives of the people inside the

organization first, to sacrifice their [own] comforts and sacrifice the tangible results so that the people remain and feel safe and that they belong, remarkable things happen. . . . If the conditions are wrong, we are forced to expend our own time and energy to protect ourselves from each other, and that inherently weakens the organization. When we feel safe inside the organization, we will naturally combine our talents and our strengths and work tirelessly to face the dangers outside and to seize the opportunities.[8]

A passage in the Gospels that has always moved me depicts Jesus's interaction with Peter after the resurrection, in which Jesus restores Peter to his purpose (John 21). Jesus, though fully aware Peter had denied him three times prior to the crucifixion, meets Peter in his humanity, validates his worth, and restores him to his purpose. It is an inspiring example of the kind of culture good leaders create. This is what Jesus always did. He affirmed people's worth, then inspired them to live a more meaningful life. Jesus was consistently affirming, loving, and inspiring. No wonder the legacy he left and the culture he created among his disciples became the greatest spiritual movement in all of human history. Consistent leaders—those who focus on the hearts and minds of those they are leading each day—create cultures that are consistently inspired.

CONSISTENT LEADERS . . . CREATE CULTURES THAT ARE CONSISTENTLY INSPIRED.

At a big corporate place like ESPN, turnover and transition among positions is constantly occurring because a lot of people are trying to climb the corporate ladder. But when I left ESPN in 2017, *OTL* still had the same identity and unique culture as when I worked there. The greatest sports dynasties have had plenty of personnel changes, but it's their culture that creates winning systems, processes, and attitudes that are continually replicated over time. At *OTL*, the people have changed, their gifts and skill sets have changed, and the times have changed. But the culture is still the same. Bob has consistently instilled value in those he is leading. He has consistently made them feel safe and has invited them into the belonging of the unique *OTL* environment. I have a feeling that plenty of other young producers have come through the doors at *OTL* to hear Bob Ley say those same words he said to me.

▼ ▼ ▼

On June 26, 2019, I woke up to the news that The General, after forty years as an ESPN anchor, was retiring. All the emotion I felt as a young producer at ESPN, when Bob took the time to invest in me and leave a unique imprint on my life, came flooding back. At a critical time, when I was new to the industry and testing out television for the first time, Bob played a huge role in my journey at ESPN. And he did the same thing for so many other people—stars like Bomani Jones, Jemele Hill, Stephen A. Smith, Chris Broussard, and Dave Zirin, along with countless others in the mainstream. Bob gave them all opportunities before anyone else did.

The legacy The General left at ESPN was as much about empowering others in his role as a leader as it was about his truth-telling as a journalist. He always allowed others to shine, from his guests, to his producers, to his colleagues. As Jon Gordon writes in *The Carpenter*, "You and your team complete this sentence: 'I love, serve, and care because _____.' When you can complete this sentence you will become a powerful success builder."[9]

Bob understood that. He is one of the most powerful success builders I've ever encountered because of the culture that was formed out of his own love, service, and care.

PUTTING ON THE UNIFORM

Some of the best leaders are the consistent leaders . . . someone like Bob Ley who epitomized professionalism and led with both humility and excellence. With Bob, you always knew what you were going to get. You knew what the expectations were. And it was out of this consistency that a one-of-a-kind culture formed and remained. Wearing the uniform of leadership must mean being able to say, "I love, serve, and care because _____" every single day in order to develop the kind of consistency that allows healthy culture to arise. The beautiful thing is that your answer can't have anything to do with your own ego because loving, serving, and caring doesn't work that way. It entails investing in others—seeing a potential in them that they themselves don't see and coming alongside them in order to help them unleash that potential and realize their dreams.

DISCUSSING THE UNIFORM

▷ Think of an inconsistent boss or coach you've had in your life. What was his or her effect on the team or group? Did people have to walk on eggshells? What was that team's culture like?

▷ What stands out to you about Bob Ley as a leader and the culture at *OTL*? How can you replicate some of his leadership techniques in your own space of influence?

▷ In whom are you investing right now or believe you need to invest? How are you doing so, or what can you do to invest in that person?

▷ Finish this sentence: "I love, serve, and care because _____."[10] If you have a hard time answering, why? Be honest but gentle with yourself.

13

IGNITING THE FIRE WITHIN

WHAT I ADMIRED ABOUT BOB Ley was similar to what I saw in my favorite basketball player growing up, Larry Bird. The Celtics Hall of Famer was selfless on the floor yet absolutely dominated the game. Whereas someone like Michael Jordan needed to drop forty-five points in order to dominate, Larry would completely control the game while scoring only twelve points. Magic Johnson was similar to Larry, but Magic was a point guard—he was *supposed* to control the floor. Larry was a small forward, but he got everyone involved, like a point guard would, because he was such a good passer and could see the floor better than anyone else in the game. In fact, it seemed like he'd rather have a game with fifteen assists than a game with forty-five points. Yet he was a three-time NBA Most Valuable Player, two-time NBA Finals Most Valuable Player, and twelve-time NBA all-star.

You could see how valuable Larry was through how his teammates shone.

That's what makes someone a good leader.

As Simon Sinek put it, "In the military they give medals to people who are willing to sacrifice themselves so that others may gain.

In business, we give bonuses to people who are willing to sacrifice others so that we may gain. It's backward."[11]

Larry had to retire at thirty-five years old because his back gave out on him after all those early years in his career of diving after loose balls with unusual reckless abandon. He didn't need to be that kind of player and hustler. He was a superstar. But he didn't care about that. He just lived in those moments—thriving right where he was—and did whatever it took to help his team win.

Same with Bob Ley. He didn't have to attend every single meeting. He didn't have to seek out a young thirty-year-old producer and invest in him. He was a superstar and could have had a successful show without that kind of emotional and mental investment within the nooks and crannies of ESPN culture. But he did.

That doesn't mean these men were soft. Larry Bird was also one of the most passionate and hard-nosed players ever to hit the hardwood. One of the great trash-talkers of the game, he was notorious for getting inside the heads of his opponents. Just another reminder that some of the most selfless leaders can also be the most passionate. You can lead with love and grace, and be intentional in your relationships, and at the same time be hungry, dedicated, and zealous.

On the surface, passion—going after what you want—and selflessness—making sure others get what they want—should mix as well as oil and water. But Larry Bird found a way to combine the two.

I remember watching his last home game in 1992, when the Boston Celtics faced the Cleveland Cavaliers in the NBA Playoffs. It was apparent by then that Larry's back was wrecked. Yet he scored sixteen points, tallied fourteen assists, and grabbed seven rebounds—nearly a triple double—in only thirty minutes of play. The small-town "Hick from French Lick," who wanted nothing more than to shoot baskets all day, tend his Indiana farm, and fish, became a model for how to play the game of basketball as a bold leader. He was a passionate player. He was a selfless teammate. But he also had something more than passion and selflessness.

Larry Bird had heart.

Passion is essential, but it can lead to micromanaging others or trying to control the journey, whereas selflessness entails serving others and helping them become the best they can be. However, selflessness that's out of balance can lead to focusing solely on others without respecting one's own interests and well-being. The thing that brings together the two competing forces, passion and selflessness, is heart. Bob and Larry (and no, I'm not talking about the tomato and the cucumber—sorry, VeggieTales fans, I couldn't resist) epitomized heart, leading with both passion and selflessness. And because of their consistent display of heart over time, they helped to create one-of-a-kind cultures in the newsroom and on the basketball court. A collective heartbeat formed. Culture formed. The Boston Celtics had a distinct culture. *OTL* had a distinct culture.

▼ ▼ ▼

What do I mean by *heart*? Another word for it might be what psychologist Angela Duckworth calls *grit*, which has been defined as "the ability to work hard for a long period of time toward a focused goal and keep moving forward in spite of challenges, obstacles, and failures."[12] I love the longevity aspect of grit. Anyone can show heart in spurts. Anyone can be passionate and selfless in certain frames in the Rolodex that is their life. A game here or a game there. A focused and intentional year here or a year there. But what makes Bob and Larry legends is their ability to show heart and work hard for a long period of time toward their focused goal. It goes back to the actively patient farmer. Back to Drew Brees. Back to that undying pursuit of excellence and perpetual investment in the process.

During his interview with Bob on the day of his retirement,

Jeremy Schaap asked him who he was thinking about that day. The people, said Bob without hesitation. He mentioned a few high-level colleagues, then got a little emotional and concluded that he just couldn't name everyone. All the meetings Bob consistently attended, all the lunches he had with his employees, all the intentional conversations he had every day—they are a reflection of the grit that animated his leadership. Passion left unmanaged can sabotage a team, but Bob was steady in his passion. He was dependable. I believe he knew exactly what he wanted and what it would take to create an unshakable culture. He never lost sight of that goal and desire.

You can easily tell when someone has grit. Such people know *why* they're doing what they're doing and *how* they can take one step after another to reinforce their why. An inspiring why is contagious and creates culture. It's also easy to see when someone doesn't have grit. Someone who is merely going through life, working for nothing more than the next paycheck and obsessed with image and perception—what others think of them.

IF YOU LEAD WITH THE HEART, YOUR EXAMPLE INSPIRES THOSE AROUND YOU TO UNLEASH SOMETHING MORE WITHIN THEMSELVES AS WELL.

But if you can be someone with grit, if you lead with the heart, your example inspires those around you to unleash something more within themselves as well. They take risks, choose to live in a different way. Grit is contagious. It's *fun* to follow someone who has passion and yet whom you can trust not to trample you or abandon you along the way.

Not that walking in long-term grit is easy. Grit is also defined as little bits of stone or sand. Try walking with some of that in your shoe for a mile or ten. It's hard. It sometimes hurts—just look at Larry Bird's back problems. But it's not enough to show heart only in the big moments and on the mountaintops. You become a person of grit only by showing heart in the small moments and in the valleys. The greatest teacher in life is adversity.

▼ ▼ ▼

In April 2012, I had the privilege of escorting legendary Cleveland Browns running back Jim Brown around ESPN's campus as he made appearances on different shows. Jim, one of the best running backs to ever play the game and an excellent actor as well, led the Browns to an NFL title in 1964 and retired in 1965 after nine NFL seasons as the league's leading rusher. When I spent the day with him, he was seventy-six years old. He walked slowly with his cane. Football had taken its toll on his body.

At first, knowing the day would be a long one with lots of walking, and wanting to help Jim conserve his energy, I offered him assistance as we walked around campus. But it didn't take long for me to learn that Jim wanted no help whatsoever. He was determined to get wherever he needed to go on his own, no matter how long it took, no matter how seemingly in pain or tired he was. Here was a man with an unshakable spirit and drive who never lost the heart that he played with on the football field. It looked different now, but it was just as inspiring, if not more so, in his old age with wobbly knees. Jim's attitude challenged me to determinedly push through some of the frustrations in my own life and let go of the pain I was holding on to. That's what heart and grit are all about. That kind of inner fire spreads to other souls and animates them in a unique way.

I think about that day with Jim whenever I feel disappointed, stuck, or weak. It inspires me to focus ahead on the prize, move determinedly forward, and simply take one step after another. All that matters is that you're in movement. That you're focused on the goal.

I had a similar experience with another guest, this time with WWE icon Hulk Hogan. I was thrilled to have the opportunity to spend the day with the Hulk. I used to watch WWE all the time as a kid and loved watching him come out to "I Am a Real American" every time he entered the ring. I even had a pretty decent Hulk Hogan impression that got me some laughs at school. (Don't even ask me to do it on *Sports Spectrum Podcast*—it's *not* happening.)

That day at ESPN, similar to Jim Brown, Hulk was sixty-two and was coming off hip surgery when we had him on the Car Wash. He walked around campus all day with a limp but didn't care. He wanted no additional help or assistance. He was determined to get from show to show on his own. Physical ailments were not going to affect his mood, his day, or his ability to be present—to wear the uniform with grace.

Even if you're not a WWE fan or familiar with Hulk Hogan, a quick Google search will reveal that if there is one word that describes him, it's passion. His WWE persona was marked by the confidence, conviction, and charisma that passion exudes. That day with him at ESPN, I was impressed by how, as an actor, he always knew how to tap into the character he had developed with WWE. He always knew how to give people what they wanted. He turned on the "Hulkster" persona when the cameras were rolling and enthralled his audience with the passionate character he had so brilliantly cultivated over the years.

Off camera, Hulk was genuinely nice and soft spoken. He even told me his story about coming to faith in Christ. But when he switched on the character he had perfected, he pulled everyone else in and captivated the hearts of WWE fans.

Hulk Hogan had to tap into his passionate persona time and

time again. You, as a leader, have the same choice every day. The hunger for worldly success will only ignite your heart in spurts. But leading with heart all the time takes a much different kind of drive, one that transcends worldly success. It requires selflessness, service, excellence, presence, and, most importantly, love.

Larry Bird once said, "Leadership is getting players to believe in you. If you tell a teammate you're ready to play as tough as you're able to, you'd better go out there and do it. Players will see right through phony. And they can tell when you're not giving it all you've got. Leadership is diving for a loose ball, getting the crowd involved, getting other players involved. It's being able to take it as well as dish it out. That's the only way you're going to get respect from players."[13]

You can unleash your passion, or you can hide it under a bushel. You can tap into your heart, or you can coast through the day and the week toward a paycheck to support you and your family. You can get intentional and try to listen to the heartbeat of others so their passions can be unleashed as well as your own, or you can stay in your own safe, little world. The choice to lead with both passion and selflessness—with a heart that will inspire others—is up to you. It is a daily decision and commitment that you get to make. Be someone who, like Larry Bird and Bob Ley, leaves a legacy that is marked by grit.

PUTTING ON THE UNIFORM

Who are some of your favorite athletes? My guess is that many of them are beloved to you because of the inspiration they displayed on the court, the field, or the course. It's easy to tell when someone plays with heart. That person rallies not only the team but also the fan base and the city. Heart is contagious. One of the sources of fuel behind leadership is to tap into not only your own heart but, most importantly, the hearts of others. Help them feel as if they are a part of something so they know they have something unique and important to contribute. Affirm that their unique skills, gifts, and personality are a vital cog in the machine.

You can only tap into the hearts of others by creating an inspired culture. And playing inspired starts with you. It is vital to get your mind right to lead—to be a thermostat, not a thermometer, and to be aware and present instead of tunnel-visioned and destination-focused. But it's also important to get your heart in the right place. At those times when you feel as if you are just going through the motions and your days are running together, return to your *why*. Get re-centered. Dive inward and remember why you are where you are, doing what you're doing. Reflect on the journey God and life have taken you on, leading to this moment, right here, right now. Return to your why again and again to develop contagious grit that will consistently inspire your culture. Then come alongside others to unleash the passions, dreams, and desires in their hearts.

DISCUSSING THE UNIFORM

▷ What is your *why*? What brings you life and joy? What ignites your heart?

▷ Reflect on your journey. Why are you thankful to be where you are, doing what you're doing? Are you unleashing what's on your heart or hiding it under a bushel?

▷ Think about some of the people on your team. What are their dreams, passions, and desires in life? If you cannot answer this question about your own teammates, they probably do not feel known by you, or understood, or as if they have anything to offer to the team. They're likely just coasting, going through the motions. It's your job as a leader to unleash their unique dreams, passions, and desires. How can you get to know your teammates more?

▷ How can you get those around you more involved in what you're trying to do as a team? How can you use everyone's unique skills and personality to strengthen the team's direction?

14

PERSPECTIVE: PASSION'S GUIDING EYE

THE CHALLENGING THING ABOUT PASSION—which flows from the heart—is that when you're caught up in it, it is sometimes difficult to maintain *perspective*. Passionate leaders have to battle tunnel vision and obsession, where priorities get out of whack. Perspective helps leaders keep their hearts in check so they can continually elevate the right values and cultural tenets and see the bigger picture. Perspective brings necessary balance to passion. It aims the heart in the right direction and moves it in that direction consistently over time. If the heart is the engine of the car, then perspective is the steering wheel, gas pedal, and brakes. It takes all of these things for the driver of the car to steadily move toward the destination, obey traffic laws, and avoid a collision.

As passionate a broadcaster as Bob Ley was and as passionate a basketball player as Larry Bird was, they nevertheless maintained perspective. Bob knew that *Outside the Lines* did not ultimately belong to him, and Larry knew the Celtics' success would hinge upon their teamwork and culture. Each man's perspective inspired a collective heartbeat in his team because he was able to keep everyone moving in the same direction. Leaders who have perspective keep egos in check, refine motives, and tap into the diversity of each person's heart while at the same time connecting all the team members to one another.

Bad leaders, on the other hand, may be passionate, but they get caught up in their individual passion. Such leaders can begin to act more like tyrants or become tunnel-visioned or controlling in their approach. Those on their team experience that person's ego rather than his or her heart.

DEVELOPING PERSPECTIVE IS ABOUT CONSTANTLY RETURNING TO THE TWO UNDERLYING INGREDIENTS OF EXPERIENCING TRUE MEANING IN LIFE: LOVING GOD AND LOVING OTHERS.

Perspective is the key that unlocks the heart and re-centers the mind. Developing perspective is about constantly returning to the two underlying ingredients of experiencing true meaning in life: loving God and loving others. Whereas passion might entail zooming in to invest all of yourself in a particular task or moment, perspective is about zooming out and realizing that your identity does not hinge upon the results of that task or moment. Doing so frees you up to invest yourself in the next moment. When you're caught in the grip of passion, perspective can inspire a return to the importance of relationships. A return to selflessness. If you don't have perspective, it's impossible to see the whole picture.

Of the hundreds of guests I got to spend the day with at ESPN, I can't think of a person who exemplifies this journey of gaining perspective more than Darryl Strawberry. Another one of my childhood sports heroes, Darryl came to ESPN during the spring of 2009 to promote his autobiography, *Finding My Way*, which detailed both his professional baseball journey and his private journey with addiction. Recovering addicts often have incredible perspective on life because they have hit rock bottom and seen their life in shambles. Their lives, filled with suffering and battle, often awaken them to their many blessings because they come so close to losing them, whether through brushes with the law or through wounding those they love most. They come in touch with the core truths of life because their addictions force them to confront themselves and their flaws.

That day at ESPN, as we talked about our lives and our faith in between shows, Darryl Strawberry shared his story with me in brief: Eight-times all-star. Winner of four World Series. Chasing fame, glory, women, and money—but hollow inside. The emptiness Darryl experienced pursuing professional success, fame, and fortune only fueled his addiction. And his addiction ruined his baseball career, forcing him to see what was really most important in life: relationships, connection, and helping others, animated by his faith. Baseball stardom had distracted him from the best focus for his passion. Not until Darryl discovered his true purpose did he realize what he was meant to do.

Passion can cause any of us to grasp for the wrong things if we forget what is most important in life. Success in Darryl's eyes is no longer about fame and fortune. It's about something much deeper than chasing ego boosts. It's about meeting people where they are and impacting their lives—loving God and loving people. It's about going into high schools and other small venues and, by sharing the story of his brokenness, helping others find their way in the world without making the same mistakes he made.

I could tell Darryl was passionate about his mission and maintaining a wise perspective on life because, for the next few years, he continued to check up on me. Through text messages and phone calls, Darryl asked about my dad, whose alcoholism had largely shaped my life. What an honor to have someone I so deeply admired take a personal interest in me.

▼ ▼ ▼

A verse in the book of Isaiah sums up perspective perfectly: "All of us have become like one who is unclean, and all our righteous acts are like *filthy rags*; we all shrivel up like a leaf, and like the wind our sins sweep us away" (64:6, emphasis mine). This verse points out a false belief. Like many in our culture, I tend to put a lot of emphasis on actions—on what I do, what I accomplish, what I attain. Even now while working in ministry. This verse reminds me that passionately pursuing accomplishments and accolades is too narrow and shallow a focus in life. Without a deeper meaning or perspective, my attainments are like filthy rags.

Arguably, the three material things the world elevates as most important are a job, a house, and a car. But these are just filthy rags if you work your job to make more money and climb the corporate ladder so others think you're important, buy a house to impress your friends, or purchase a lavish car to catch looks from pedestrians while driving through town. A lot of these shallow pursuits are fueled by comparison and coveting. Comparison is the thief of joy.

Many people have never considered the deeper meaning and potential of what they've been given and what they are pursuing. Imagine the possibilities when love shapes your perspective. What if you see your office as a space to connect with others, hear what your employees are passionate about, validate their worth, and inspire them as they pursue their purpose in life? Suddenly your job becomes a temple. Similarly, when you view your house as a place to host Bible studies, raise a family, gather people together, or lend a room to someone who is struggling in life, then your house becomes a temple. And if see your car as something that enables you to volunteer at the homeless shelter, make memories with your family at the beach, or listen to podcasts or music during your drive time that help you grow into a more loving individual, then your car becomes a temple. See how a little perspective changes everything?

If I had twenty Emmys but didn't impact a single soul, then what's the point of an Emmy? You can't take it with you when you die. No one will be impressed by your television award in heaven. At ESPN, people always had their Emmys on display in their offices. Don't get me wrong—it was cool. But what's the point of any trophy or accolade or promotion or raise if you run over others on the way to obtaining it? If you abandon your family in the process? Candidly, there were times when I myself lost perspective of loving God and loving others, and ESPN became the god in my life that I worshiped. As a consequence, my home life was affected. My relationships with friends were affected. My relationship with *myself* was affected. No amount of success at work makes up for failure at home or in your relationships.

What's funny is that I actually have an Emmy. And, to my point, as hard as I worked at ESPN, and as passionate and dedicated as I was to climb and to grab hold of my dreams, I got my Emmy for almost no reason at all. Really. When a team at ESPN submitted *SportsCenter* as the show they wanted to be up for an Emmy back in 2004, I was working as a talent producer for *Outside the Lines*. There were two spots for talent producers on their submission. But though I had booked several guests for *SportsCenter* through my work at *OTL*, I was far from a full-time talent producer at *SportsCenter*. They wrote my name down regardless, probably because of the limited booking work I had done for the show.

After we found out that *SportsCenter* was going to receive an

Emmy that year for being the best studio show, I received a call from a coworker. "Hey, congrats, you won an Emmy!" he said.

"I did?"

"Yeah, your name was on the *SportsCenter* list."

"That's right. I totally forgot about that."

And that's how I became an Emmy Award–winning producer.

The story shocks people sometimes when I share it, but I love it because it echoes everything I've been talking about in this chapter. My Emmy Award might sit on the mantel in my living room, but it's just a trophy. Just a hunk of metal. Something I did not even deserve to win.

I've talked to a number of Super Bowl champions who don't even know where their Super Bowl rings are. What they *do* remember are the locker room prayers, the conversations in their hotel rooms about family or faith or their struggles in life, and the laughs they shared with friends. They remember how they grew as a person while pursuing their professional football dreams. They remember the heartbeat of their culture. They remember those loving moments, those deep relationships, that they experienced with their teammates or in the community. They remember their experiences with *people* that made the ride special.

PUTTING ON THE UNIFORM

In the last chapter we talked about the importance of continually tapping into your why and igniting all that resides within your heart—and most importantly, the hearts of others—in order to create an inspired culture. But to protect yourself from letting your passion misguide you, which can create an unhealthy intensity or unrealistic expectations within your culture, it's important to maintain perspective. It's your job, as a leader, to always see the bigger picture. It's your job to see the deeper meaning and significance of things—even in failure. Cultivating perspective will help those you are leading not to take failure too personally, and it will inspire them to keep trying new things. As a leader, it's your responsibility to make every aspect of your life a sacred space for something deeper to be birthed and to unfold.

DISCUSSING THE UNIFORM

▷ Talk about a time when you got too caught up in your passion or desire and lost touch with reality. What woke you up? How did you get re-centered?

▷ Reflect upon your favorite sports team that you played on, your favorite department you worked in, or your favorite group in the workplace. What do you remember about that experience? What made it such a good experience: successes or something deeper? How can you replicate that experience today?

▷ How can you turn your office, house, car, or other space where your life unfolds into a sanctuary of depth and meaning?

15

BE BOLD, BE BRAVE

PERSPECTIVE NOT ONLY HELPS YOU focus on the most important things, but it can free you up to be bold and brave—to no longer be controlled by fear but to do what you believe is right. We humans tend to lean too much into fear. We imagine all that can go wrong if we put ourselves out there—how foolish we might look, how we might fail to meet our own or other people's expectations. As a result, we don't risk pursuing what is really on our hearts.

A bit of perspective can open up our heart and take the sting out of failure. Perspective puts our fear in context and helps us see what is really important so we can be bold, brave, and true to whatever we are supposed to do to positively impact our sphere of influence.

I love this verse from the book of Joshua: "Have I not commanded you? Be strong and courageous. Do not be afraid; do not be discouraged, for the LORD your God will be with you wherever you go" (1:9). Perspective, zooming out, creates the cognitive space for us to zoom back in and share what is on our hearts. Resting in the reality that God is always with us—in success and in failure, when life is unfolding smoothly and when it involves managing stress or

taking risks—can free us up in our hearts and minds to be strong
and courageous, bold and brave.

I was fortunate to have some really good bosses at ESPN, and
two in particular lived out this kind of boldness and bravery. I
learned something unique about leadership from each of them. One,
a young gun named Gabe Goodwin, miraculously went from being
an associate producer at twenty-seven to a coordinating producer at
thirty. That's jumping a level every single year, which, believe me,
is not common at ESPN. It takes someone special to stand out like
that.

My first time working with Gabe was indirectly for a *Sports-
Nation* show that unveiled the cover of the Madden football video
game. I knew right away that he was one of a kind. He was confident
but never arrogant. He toed that line. When you talk about setting a
temperature, he was one of those guys: secure in his convictions and
confident in his approach. He made you feel like you could follow
him anywhere, perhaps against the grain but anywhere nonetheless,
all the while knowing that you were seen and heard.

I once helped Gabe at another Madden cover reveal show, and
he took the time to send me a personal note thanking me for how
I handled things during a stressful situation for the producers. It
was that day, I believe, that ultimately led to my working for him a
year later when he gave me an opportunity in ESPN's social media
department. His being eight years younger than me didn't matter;
he had my full respect. He was much different from me personality-
wise, but he was a professional and one of the most motivated people
I had encountered. He was someone I had a lot to learn from.

I believe it was Gabe's boldness and bravery that helped him
climb as fast as he did. Sure, he ruffled some feathers, but he stuck
to his convictions and was determined to do what he felt was right
for the company based on what he was seeing in the industry and on
his study of the marketing trends. See, just doing what you think is

right might make you bold and brave in a certain sense, but making sure that what you believe to be true is calculated—tested through trial and error, critiqued by others, weighed with conflicting opinions, and approached with perspective—is what will give you more credibility when you step out.

Gabe's biggest contribution to ESPN's culture, I believe, was his influence in the social media world. Crazy as it might sound today, he and I were both working at ESPN at a time when social media was not a priority for mainstream media. In the first decade of the 2000s, Twitter, for example, was believed to be a fad. Just like Myspace was a fad.

BOLD LEADERS AREN'T INTERESTED IN JUST BLENDING IN; THEY'RE FOCUSED ON MAKING A DIFFERENCE AND LETTING THEIR VOICES BE HEARD.

Gabe was one of the first to speak up and tell his superiors that social media was a legitimate thing, and we needed to use it to our advantage. On *SportsNation*, for example, he was testing things that no one else was doing, conducting live Twitter polls during the show, displaying athletes' tweets for viewers, and giving the audience an opportunity to interact with hosts via social media and possibly be mentioned on air. He was putting a dent in the comfortable world that was ESPN television—trying something new, which takes boldness. Gabe was tampering with a well-oiled machine, but he had the foresight to know he had to tamper in order to stay ahead of the innovation curve.

He was exactly right. Within a couple years, other ESPN shows and even programs at other networks were replicating the format of

SportsNation, integrating social media and audience interaction into their coverage.

When I started working for Gabe, I was excited to come under the tutelage of a true visionary and help put social media at ESPN on the map when it was still in its infancy. It was the journey of a lifetime. Gabe had the boldness to stand up and get people to pay attention to something he thought was important. Not everyone listened to him at first, but he kept following his convictions, within reason, and in my opinion ultimately sparked a movement that forever changed television. It didn't matter that he was young. It didn't matter that he was relatively new to ESPN. He was a bold leader. And bold leaders aren't interested in just blending in; they're focused on making a difference and letting their voices be heard.

▼ ▼ ▼

Another bold leader I had the privilege of working under for several years as a talent producer was Lisa Stokes, a tough, sharp, and perfectionistic Boston woman who made a splash at ESPN through her work ethic and innovation on the talent-producing side. I watched her navigate the world of management with grace and determination. Lisa was firm and tough but also loving and tender. She pushed us to be the best we could be in the workplace but also saw us as friends and confidants in life.

Not only was Lisa a bold leader in the professional space, she was also a brave leader in her personal life—and in *our* personal lives. In 2012, she and I started having lots of conversations about faith, and these talks impacted both of us on a profound level. Not long after, she and her husband started coming to the church in Bristol where Dawn and I attend. And soon afterward, she approached me after church and asked what I thought about her starting a fellowship group at ESPN. I thought it was a great idea, and before I knew it, the group was off and running. Typical Lisa. When she sets her mind to something, it doesn't take long for that thing to get put into motion in an excellent way.

Her vision for the group was that it would be a place for ESPN employees to come every other Thursday during their lunch break and connect with others who were curious about having conversations about faith and spirituality. It would be a time for people to come together and pray, share their struggles with one another, read Scripture, and occasionally listen to guest speakers share their testimonies. The group debuted in August 2014, and I still have the picture. There are eight of us in that group photo along with legendary college football coach Bobby Bowden, who just happened to be visiting that day. He swung by our group and shared an encouraging word with us.

The group continued for nearly a half decade, a rock in people's lives that they could return to and re-center themselves amid the chaos of the workweek and the pressures at ESPN. The group was a constant encouragement to me, and, from a leadership perspective, I found it to be a beautiful reflection of the person Lisa is. When she sets her mind to something, there is no holding her back. She continued to build the group's infrastructure over the years, tapping into her network of people to come and share their testimonies—people like NBA analyst Chris Broussard and football players Brian Dawkins and Jeff Saturday. Even best-selling author Bob Goff took time to share with our little ESPN group.

Lisa didn't have to take the time and energy to organize the group twice a month for several years and tap into her own resources. But she saw people at ESPN as so much more than coworkers or employees. They were *people* who carried with them burdens and sufferings. Creating a space for deep connection would not only help them realize they weren't alone and could confide in their ESPN family, but it would also make them healthier mentally and emotionally in the workplace. Lisa saw the depths of individuals.

What made her efforts even braver was that she wasn't a Bible scholar, a minister, or a church leader. In fact, she was a brand-new Christian when she started the group. Some people think they need a degree or years of leadership experience to make an impact on the rich, deep parts of people's lives, but that couldn't be further from the truth. All it takes to create connection is one person who wants to serve and bring people together. If that person steps out, not fearing what other respected leaders might think, he or she can change an entire group of people. Brave leaders don't apologize for who they are. They are just themselves. And they make a space for others to be themselves as well, and to share what is on their hearts and minds.

Putting on the Uniform

Maintaining perspective in your leadership will free you and others up to be bold and brave—to have the courage to try new things and not be afraid of failure. To go after something with all your heart, even if that entails making mistakes, and learn valuable lessons along the way. If those you are leading are afraid to make a mistake, then it's your job as a leader to help them develop a perspective that will liberate them to take risks and even fail along the way—because that is what is going to lead to the most growth.

It's up to you to create a culture of excellence, not a culture of fear. Do something exciting. Pave a new path. And don't let what the world may say about your education, experience, or age discourage you from following your convictions and learning along the way.

DISCUSSING THE UNIFORM

▷ Do you make decisions out of fear or love? A fear of failure or a love for what you get to do in life?

▷ Where in your life could you use more boldness and bravery? Develop some perspective? What's the worst thing that could happen?

▷ Do those you are entrusted to lead make bold and brave decisions? Or are they timid and fearful? Evaluate your culture. Highlight what is good about it and think of ways you can improve it. How can you empower others to be bold and brave—to try new things unhindered by fear of failure? What conversations do you need to have with individuals in order to free up their hearts and minds—to take risks and grow on the adventure you're all embarking on together?

16

MILK JUGS AND ANCHORMEN

In my childhood, I witnessed my dad's joyous tears and childlike exhilaration whenever one of his favorite professional teams won a game. But I also saw his rage whenever his team lost. Whenever his New York Giants, St. Louis Cardinals, or Boston Celtics struggled, there were usually cursing tirades and absurd threats. He once threw a plant at the wall, shattering the clay pot. Much as I loved sports myself, it always shocked me that Dad took these losses so personally. After all, it was just a game. Something he had no control over. Something to be enjoyed. I didn't realize at the time that his outbursts were almost always alcohol related. Nonetheless, he took sports *very* seriously.

Perhaps you, too, know someone who takes sports just a little too seriously. Someone you don't want to be around if their team loses. Someone who is way too desperate for victory and way too broken after a loss. I'm thankful to say my dad is no longer that way. He and I have enjoyed a number of games in person together since he got sober a few years ago. I really enjoy watching games with him now. We have even gone to a Celtics game together at The Garden in Boston and a Cardinals game at Busch Stadium in St. Louis.

Sports can be a great release that is fun and entertaining and that brings people together. But taken too seriously, it can cause suffering because of people's unhealthy attachment to their favorite team.

Life is the same way. Each day is filled with different outlets that can and should be enjoyed. Yet we can easily turn them into avenues of pain by making them bigger than they really are. Our goals and problems aren't meant to be torture chambers. Whether we're at work, or creating something meaningful, or playing sports, or coaching a team, our activities should give us satisfaction, not stress us out because we take them and ourselves too seriously.

A key psychological benefit of keeping perspective is that it helps us laugh at our mistakes, have fun and smile as we go about our day, and refrain from beating ourselves up. Life undoubtedly has challenges and frustrations, and sometimes they truly are serious. But often we give them too much weight. It's our choice whether we'll allow ordinary hassles to affect us mentally and emotionally. We can have grace for ourselves, or we can judge ourselves; we can laugh at ourselves, or we can shame ourselves; we can learn from our mistakes, or we can brood over what we can't change.

GOOD LEADERS REALIZE THAT FAILURE IS PART OF THE JOURNEY, AND THEY DON'T NEED TO FEAR FAILURE.

Unfortunately, I often approach life and work the way my dad approached sports in my childhood: I take too seriously things that should be enjoyed. One of the cornerstones of the Christian faith is grace: love from God that we could never deserve. It's God's free gift to us through his Son—yet I sometimes struggle to experience God's love and grace in daily living. I can be so critical of myself, both in how I handle life's details and just overall. A lot of that comes from having unhealthy attachments in life. I try to control things a little too much. Check that: *way* too much. You too, maybe? We stress and suffer needlessly as a result.

Good leaders can pursue excellence and *enjoy* that pursuit. They can zoom in and focus on the task at hand, but they can also zoom out and realize that the task and their performance in handling it do not define them. That goes back to perspective. It frees up good leaders to remain a thermostat even when they experience failure. It empowers them to keep moving forward with grit even when something unfolds imperfectly. They simply take the next step and invest themselves in the next process—and, most importantly, in the people in that process. Good leaders realize that failure is part of the journey, and they don't need to fear failure.

Jon Gordon says it well:

> We all fail. . . . It's what we do after we fail that determines what we build in the long run. Some of the most successful people throughout history have experienced great failures, but they turned their great failures into great success. Most people don't know that Walt Disney was once fired from a newspaper for a lack of ideas, and his first cartoon production company went bankrupt. . . . And it's easy to forget that Steve Jobs was fired from Apple at 30 years old, and that Oprah Winfrey was fired as a news anchor and told she wasn't fit for television.[14]

Failure is a gift. It can strengthen our direction. It can bring clarity in our processes. It can give us perspective. It can ignite growth and transformation. Failure doesn't have to be feared.

Yes, there is failure in sports, and there is failure in life. But at the end of the day, both sports and life should be fun and enjoyable.

Leaders get to decide whether they will enjoy the journey in their pursuit of excellence.

▼ ▼ ▼

There were times when I took my career way too seriously, took rejection and failure way too personally, and became borderline obsessed with the next step, consumed with how others perceived me. But then would come a slap-in-the-face reminder that work at ESPN, as much as it was about excellence and being the best sports media company on the planet, was also about having fun. Two such occasions were the days when New England Patriots tight end Rob Gronkowski and superstar comedian Will Ferrell visited Bristol.

"Gronk," who came for the Car Wash in 2015, was like a big ole kid the entire day. Even though he worked his butt off on the gridiron and was part of an organization that epitomized excellence (the Patriots have won six Super Bowl titles, nine AFC championships, and sixteen AFC East titles since Belichick took over in 2000), you could tell Gronk just wanted to have a good time at ESPN. You could tell he loved his lifestyle and all the fun things that came with it.

That day, Gronk, notorious for how he spiked the football whenever he scored a touchdown, let us film a segment where he spiked different objects we gave him. A gallon of milk. A pineapple. A trophy. Many athletes won't go along with these ridiculous media bits and sketches because of how silly a person might end up looking, but Gronk didn't care. He just wanted to have fun. He was the life of the party all day long.

That's not to say *you* have to be the life of the party in order to have a lighthearted approach to life. Just have fun in whatever way fits your personality. In Gronk's case, his radical enjoyment of life and his go-with-the-flow embrace of new experiences stood out as a reminder that we're all created to live life to the fullest (John 10:10).

▼ ▼ ▼

Whereas Gronk might've been the most entertaining guest I ever experienced during my time as a talent producer, Will Ferrell was the funniest. Will came to ESPN in conjunction with the release of the 2008 sports comedy *Semi-Pro* and filmed a number of segments in his ridiculous ABA warmup suit, including one for Jim Rome's show that you can watch on YouTube.[15] Will has been known to do the unexpected: change into a red coat in the middle of a Lakers game to match the Staples Center security; host an episode of *SportsCenter* as Ron Burgundy, the dimwitted local television host from the movie *Anchorman*. In typical Will Ferrell fashion, he came to ESPN on a Saturday.

Not a ton goes on at ESPN during the weekend. Other than *SportsCenter*, the big shows air on the weekdays. So that Saturday was predictably quiet—until Will arrived. He had ESPN to himself. He wreaked havoc for three hours with his improvised, slapstick humor. Like Hulk Hogan, he amazed me with how easily and flawlessly he could click into character without ever cracking a smile at the ridiculous things he said.

Fun and enjoyment should be cornerstones of our lives. Sure, challenges come with each workday. Stresses emerge. Trials. Temptations to react, to beat ourselves up for our mistakes, to stress out when expectations aren't met. But overall, every day I worked at ESPN held hundreds of things to enjoy. After all, I've spent my career in sports, an industry built on fun, enjoyment, and entertainment.

Of course, we have to learn to come up for air—to let go and surrender whatever it is we are clinging to and trying to control. This is important in every aspect of life. For example, I've finally learned that in watching my daughter play softball, it's much more important for me to just enjoy watching the game and let her go through the growth process on her own rather than yelling my advice from the sidelines. This makes the game more fun for her, and conversations are better on the way home.

Relationships are cultivated in fun, healthy environments, and teamwork thrives when people enjoy each other's company. The best leaders understand this. So while they recognize the challenges, deadlines, and high-stress situations, they also make space for those they lead to lighten up and enjoy themselves. That approach helps cultivate healthy living, mentally and emotionally, for each individual; and collectively, it animates excellence and enhances an inspiring culture. There's synergy and excitement. People look forward to coming to work or to practice.

The different events in every day can be reminders of God's love and grace if we open our eyes to the positive possibilities.

PUTTING ON THE UNIFORM

Being bold and brave enough to pursue excellence, to try something new, can be a heavy weight to carry. Having a lighthearted perspective frees the people you lead to fail and make mistakes on the way. The pursuit of your goals will be demanding and incredibly challenging at times, but it should also be marked by fun and enjoyment, laughter, and even foolishness. If an athlete puts on his uniform but doesn't enjoy playing the game, then what's the point? If a fan watches a game but doesn't enjoy it—if he or she is just anxious the entire time—what's the point?

God's love and grace, which is always abundant in every space where our lives unfold, should always evoke enjoyment and transformation. Similarly, your job as a leader is to cultivate both joy and development. Relationships will flourish in a culture built on enjoyment. You'll make more memories. Dive in and give your all in the pursuit of excellence, but don't be afraid to zoom out and laugh at yourself along the way.

DISCUSSING THE UNIFORM

▷ What areas of your life do you tend to take too seriously, judging yourself and others harshly? What do you become too attached to, causing you to suffer in your desire to control that aspect of your life?

▷ Lighten up and laugh at yourself. You're not perfect, and God, who *is* perfect, doesn't expect you to be. So make a habit of having grace for yourself. Reflect on a funny mistake you made, turn it into a nutty story, and share it with someone. Practice lightheartedness.

▷ How has failure been a gift to you? How has it helped you in your growth and development? Give an example.

▷ Do people laugh and have fun in the different environments of your life? Why or why not? How can you help create a culture that cultivates joy and development?

17

BIG-TIME EMPATHY

THIS BOOK BEGAN WITH MY struggle to bloom where I was planted. To wear the uniform I'd been given for the team I was on. I was so preoccupied with getting to where I felt I needed to be that I had lost focus on where I was. As a result, I neglected the relationships I could invest in that were right at hand. Passion for my personal career goals blinded me to the beauty around me—the meaningful space where God had creatively led me; the culture smack in front of me where I had an opportunity to love, serve, and show empathy to others. I needed a dose of perspective.

Thank goodness for Jessica and Coach Dungy. They helped me see the importance of showing up with everything I am, right where I am. That principle applies to every leader. Because whether it's in the workplace, our team, our household, or wherever we spend our time, there are usually people in these places. And people have depth.

The secretary who answers the phone in your office isn't simply a secretary. He or she is a person. Someone on a journey. Perhaps a spouse. Perhaps a father or mother. Most certainly a friend. And he or she will inevitably bring the difficulties and stresses of life into the workplace.

The manager on your basketball team is not simply someone who cleans the gym, fills up the water bottles, or brings you a towel. He or she is someone who is trying to figure things out in life. A person with real emotions and dreams, made in the image of God, with something you can learn that will inspire you on your own journey.

Your boss or coach is not simply someone who is trying to turn a profit or win a championship; that person is someone with insecurities, challenges at home, hobbies, and passions.

POSITION YOURSELF TO MEET OTHERS IN THEIR STRUGGLES, SHARE THEIR JOYS, LISTEN TO THEM, SERVE THEM, AND HELP TO EMPOWER THEM ON THEIR JOURNEY.

By choosing to thrive in your present circumstances, you position yourself to meet others in their struggles, share their joys, listen to them, serve them, and help to empower them on their journey. You have the opportunity to share life with others and empathize with them—to understand their personalities, pressures, and struggles in life so you can offer them grace, compassion, and understanding. You can reassure them that they are not alone. They have their leader in their corner.

Not everyone cares to share their trials and difficulties. Some people want to keep their lives compartmentalized. But empathy breaks down compartmentalizing. A good leader, a servant-leader, is willing to go beyond the workplace and dig deeper than the surface. It's up to you, as that kind of leader, to break through the invisible wall that exists between work and the rest of life. Because everyone is going through something the rest of us know nothing about.

When you show those you lead that you care about their entire lives, both at work and outside of work, you show them value. That kind of care could have nothing to do with work. It could have nothing to do with turning a profit or winning championships.

Jesus understood this. When Pilate sought a worldly label to describe him based on his societal status, Jesus responded, "You say that I am a king. In fact, the reason I was born and came into the world is to testify to the truth" (John 18:37). Pilate, in his compartmentalized world, was attempting to categorize Jesus; but Jesus, coming from another world entirely, heaven, saw this world far more clearly. He saw the futility in labels and worldly status and simply wanted to show others love and empathy so they, too, could get beneath the surface and live deeper, more fulfilling lives.

Human beings have hearts and minds, spirits and souls, struggles and joys, insecurities and power, and they carry every aspect of themselves with them wherever they go. Therefore, wherever people are, you have an opportunity to be a great leader. If you're working to put on the uniform of leadership every day, you will care about what you're doing and whom you are serving.

▼ ▼ ▼

The best boss I've ever had, Carol Voronyak, demonstrated these concepts to me daily at ESPN. Carol beat me out of a job at a time when I was doing some intense soul searching, not long after I received my poor midyear review. Desperate to move up at ESPN and climb the corporate ladder, I had applied to be manager of all ESPN talent producers. Carol applied as well and got the job. I was frustrated; I felt my longevity at ESPN should have given me a leg up on other candidates. Besides, I was thirty-three and she was only twenty-six. I swallowed my pride, however, and told her, "I support you fully and will do whatever you need me to do."

Turns out Carol was the perfect hire and would impact me in profound ways the remainder of my time at ESPN.

One Christmas, Carol gave each of us a lengthy, very genuine note that highlighted what she was thankful for in us as individuals. It really moved me and was perhaps the nicest thing I ever received from a coworker at ESPN. She then gave each of us five talent producers a package of blank cards, and she encouraged us to write one another a similar note saying specifically what we were thankful for in each recipient. Participation wasn't mandatory, but Carol had already set the tone through her own notes. She also challenged us to name something about each person that went deeper than the workplace—something about that individual's personality or values, or a specific circumstance or memory that moved us on a deep level.

The intentionality behind the exercise led to something truly special. I held on to the notes my coworkers gave me and still have them today. Carol went out of her way to see each of us, recognize us as valued people, and empathize with where we were at. In turn, with her authenticity on full display, everyone did the exercise. Those cards reminded us of how we were blooming. They rooted us in the present. They forced us to take ourselves out of the equation and focus all our energy on the person to whom we were writing.

I don't know anyone who doesn't benefit from words of affirmation. The best teams have people who affirm one another and also seek wise counsel and feedback on how they can improve.

Throughout my time in the media industry, I have had plenty of bosses who cared only about work, not the person. But not Carol. Her intentionality, awareness, and empathy for each of us and our personal situations created a culture that was intimate and family-like. So many of my workplace relationships were transactional rather than transformational. But Carol wanted each of us to transform and all of us to grow close as a team, as a family, as a cohesive unit moving forward together.

No surprise, years later, that it was Carol who allowed me to switch my hours and come to work earlier so I could pick my daughter up from school and spend extra time with her at a formative period of her life. No other talent producer was working my hours, but Carol understood my request. She saw me as so much more than what I could do for her or how I could make her shine professionally. She saw me for the person I am and the life I lived. I was more than a talent producer; I was also a husband and a father and a friend. And Carol understood that if she could validate those other aspects of who I am, I would be a *better* talent producer and a more well-rounded and dedicated ESPN employee. Her empathy showed me plainly that she was in my corner and wanted me to excel both in and outside the workplace. When I left ESPN, in my goodbye note, I wrote, "To the best boss I've ever had, Carol Voronyak."

▼ ▼ ▼

When then Stanford University head football coach Jim Harbaugh came to ESPN in conjunction with a PAC 10 Coaches' Car Wash, he asked me question after question between shows. He was incredibly inquisitive. It was almost as if he didn't realize that I was there to serve him and make sure his day went smoothly. He just wanted to know more about me and my life. After filming a segment for a show, he would return to me and continue our conversation exactly where we had left off. I was amazed by both his memory and his presence. He was ESPN's guest of honor that day, yet he made the day more about me!

New York Mets legend Dwight "Doc" Gooden was similar. Doc, like Darryl Strawberry, was one of my childhood sports heroes. And also like Darryl, he saw addiction wreck his career. He was having a difficult time when I was writing this book, but nothing can erase Doc's impact on me the day he came to ESPN. His amazing openness with me about his story created a space between us for me to open up about my own struggle to forgive my alcoholic father. He helped me understand some of the nuances of addiction—and he even asked for my dad's phone number. My dad, a huge baseball fan, was absolutely floored when he got a call from Doc Gooden, a baseball legend. Doc helped me to have more empathy for my dad—to be more curious about the complexities of addiction rather than focused on judging him. Each of us, as leaders, has the opportunity to be more empathetic and curious toward others and their stories.

Our culture has gotten away from relationships and become self-absorbed in our own wants and needs. In our personal ambitions and desires. Self-centeredness, however, doesn't produce empathy. It leads to isolation and loneliness, comparison and conceit. Qualities that produce the worst types of leaders. Such leaders always end up empty and wanting more. What they grab hold of is never enough.

In *Lead . . . for God's Sake!*, one of the main characters, Coach, gets too caught up in trying to win another state championship. When one of his starters quits midseason, telling Coach that he is going through a lot and needs to focus on his family, Coach immediately gets upset. Instead of getting curious about his player's situation, he accuses the man of selfishness. Later he finds out that his player's parents were going through a divorce and the responsibility fell on his player to take care of his siblings—the exact opposite of selfishness.

Years before, Coach had gotten into coaching to make an impact on young men. But his empathy that season had gotten lost in his ambition. He forgot what coaching—and life—was all about.

The character trait that will heal the rampant division in our culture, cure toxic workplace environments, and stop the dehumanization of others is a dedication to empathy—knowing, understanding, and serving others as we form deep relationships with them.

When Carol's mother was sick, her superiors did for her what she did for me in positioning me to spend more time with my daughter. They allowed her to work from home from her mother's bedside for several months. No guilt. No shame. No transaction. They told her to do whatever she needed to and reassured her that they were in her corner. Their empathy and understanding made her an even more passionate and dedicated employee.

When my grandfather, George Romano, passed away in 2007, the entire talent-producing staff sent me flowers to put on Pa's grave. I can't tell you how much it meant to me to know that my coworkers were thinking of me on one of the hardest days of my life.

A little bit of empathy changes everything. It always has and always will. Especially in a culture that is becoming increasingly self-serving, empathy stands out. The empathy you show as a leader will create a ripple effect that, like those Christmas note cards, spreads throughout your company or team.

▼ ▼ ▼

On my last day at ESPN in 2017, I came to work feeling thankful for the journey ESPN had welcomed me into. I don't think I fully understood the transition I was about to go through—the risk involved in my leap into full-time ministry—but my heart was full. During those seventeen years at ESPN, I had learned so much about myself, what true success really is, and what it means to wear my uniform well. To bloom where I was planted. Thanks to ESPN and all the incredible people there, I am who I am today.

During my last year at ESPN, I worked for *Mike and Mike in the Morning* as their social media director. Carol had been the one who, years before, suggested my talents might align well as a social media producer, a position that changed everything for me and freed me up even more to be with my family. Once again, she saw me as so much more than just a means to elevate herself; she had my interests and family in mind. The move ultimately led to my position on *Mike & Mike*—perfect for my schedule and, interestingly, one of the shows where my career at ESPN had begun back in 2000. The show in those days was nothing like the phenomenon it had become. It had grown from a small, grungy radio room to a massive, open, high-ceilinged television studio that not only broadcasted on radio, podcast, web, and XM radio platforms but also simulcasted on television every morning for four hours on ESPN 2. I loved working on *Mike & Mike* once more.

At the end of my last show on my last day at ESPN, Mike Greenburg and Mike Golic, the hosts of the show known to most as "Greeny" and "Golic," did something I never expected. They paused the show and asked the producers to pan the main camera over to me. Greeny then introduced the audience to me, as I worked mostly behind the scenes. "Today is the last day, not only with us but at ESPN, for someone who has been here just about as long as we have," Greeny said. "He worked on our show fifteen years ago, and then came back in the last year to work with us as our social media director. The one thing I will say about him, of the many that you could, is that he is the one thing in life that we need more of. He is a genuinely nice person, and he's done a great job for us. . . . He has a great passion for sports, but he has an even greater passion for his faith, and he is following that in his next professional endeavor."

Golic added, "That's an incredible person who can leave what he has done for so long because he feels that he has another calling."[16]

They didn't have to do that. I had worked with them a decade and a half before but had only been with them for a year my second time around. They had nothing to gain in highlighting me. But they did anyway. More than that, they focused on who I was—my personality and my faith—rather than what I did for them. Going out of one's way to show someone else how important they are to them creates a ripple effect that can potentially travel into every corner of a company or culture.

It was a benediction that perfectly represented my time at ESPN. At every step along the way, I had witnessed the value so many leaders gave to those they led. One might think that at the Worldwide Leader in Sports—the top sports media company in the world—the daily environment would be intense, cutthroat, and focused on the bottom line. And sure, like any company, it was all of those things at times. But what I consistently experienced in that environment was an awakening to my true value and worth, thanks to the leaders who guided me. I am thankful to have learned from leaders who truly bloomed where they were planted—such as Greeny and Golic in the empathy they displayed on my final day at ESPN.

"Now," Greeny concluded, "make sure you steal multiple things on your way out."

PUTTING ON THE UNIFORM

Your legacy of leadership may well be defined by how empathetic you are. Empathy connects us to one another. It cultivates deep relationships. I've often heard that at the end of the day people remember how you made them feel. Leadership absolutely requires challenging those you lead, pushing them, and helping them to develop, but if you don't make people feel valued and inspired, then you probably are not a good leader. Remember: When you take the field, you represent something that is much bigger than yourself. And empathy holds everything together. It is the glue to relationships— relationships that are vital to the culture you're creating and, most importantly, vital to each person's sense of purpose in life. Empathy breeds connectedness.

DISCUSSING THE UNIFORM

▷ How can you implement strategies that challenge people to see the depth of their teammates and have gratitude for their individual gifts and skills, like Carol did with her team?

▷ Are you dedicated to knowing, understanding, and serving others? Do you want to form deep relationships with those you are leading? If yes, how do your actions and attitudes show it? If no, why not?

▷ Discuss a time when someone in a leadership position expressed empathy toward you and your circumstance. What impact did that have on you? Have you ever had a boss or a coach who was dedicated to knowing you and understanding what was going on in your life? If so, how did that make you feel?

▷ What is going on in the lives of those you are leading right now? What are their struggles and concerns? How are they doing in their personal lives? Do they feel comfortable sharing these things with you? Why or why not?

18

SMALL SEEDS OF GREAT PURPOSE

SINCE I STARTED WORKING AT Sports Spectrum in 2017, I have gotten close to a number of minor league baseball players who are connected to our parent organization, Pro Athletes Outreach. PAO serves a lot of these minor leaguers, equipping them with opportunities for mentorship and resources for discipleship.

It has been interesting to witness the environments at the different minor league levels. In Single A, there are usually a lot of guys who are young and hopeful, hungry and optimistic that they will one day make it to the majors. In Double A, that vibe is still mostly prevalent. But then in Triple A, there is a palpable discouragement and even despair in locker room cultures. Triple A baseball consists of guys on Major League Baseball's doorstep who have often put years and years of hard work into their journey. Many of them have had close calls with the majors or even short stints subbing on a major league team before being sent back down to the minors once the regular player returned from his injury or suspension. Imagine being on the brink of achieving your dream but experiencing rejection time and time again. Imagine how excruciating and heartbreaking that would be. I've noticed a callousness and fatigue prevalent in players' attitudes at this level. Many of them are beginning to accept that they might not reach the majors after all.

Contrary to what a lot of people think, being a professional baseball player is *not* glamorous if you're not in the majors. I recently featured a pitcher named Caleb Frare on the *Sports Spectrum Podcast*, and he shared some eye-opening stories with our audience about eight guys sharing a one-bedroom apartment. No one could afford to get his own, nor could any of them afford to sign a lease individually since they could get relocated any day. And the daily thirty-dollar food stipend on the road simply went toward purchasing an ungodly amount of Subway sandwiches, peanut butter, jelly, and a loaf of bread to fill their stomachs with carbs and protein so they'd have energy for the game that night. Not exactly the optimal diet that a lot of superstar athletes follow.

Perhaps you can relate to being somewhere that is not ideal . . . or feeling lost in the desert, unsure which direction to go . . . or having a boss who causes you stress and anxiety . . . or being unable to attain your dreams no matter how hard you try.

What's the point? Is there a deeper purpose? Why?

I believe the answer to those three questions is *blooming and thriving*.

Wearing the uniform of leadership the right way, loving and serving right where you are.

▼ ▼ ▼

When I first started working at Sports Spectrum, I had a minor leaguer named Ethan Chapman write a fifteen-part blog series for our website about his journey in the minor leagues playing for a Triple A team in Mexico. His experience was similar to Caleb's, filled with hopeful opportunities and heartbreaking disappointments, close calls with the team's major league affiliate and desert phases in the minors. At twenty-eight years old, Ethan ultimately decided to retire from the game and focus on being a husband and father while working at a sports agency.

In the world's eyes, Ethan might appear a failure because he never made it to the majors. But in his eyes, he had made it further in his professional baseball journey than 99 percent of those who ever seriously played the game. He wrote about how the challenges he encountered in the minors helped him develop the internal qualities of fortitude, hope, commitment, and leadership that his journey as a spouse and a parent required.

It's all about perspective.

It's all about seeing the bigger picture.

It's all about reframing your view of the harvest.

Another minor leaguer I've had the opportunity to know and interview is Jake Reed, a pitcher who has been grinding away in Triple A with the Minnesota Twins organization for the last three years—laboring and planting seeds hoping something will grow. Despite his solid performances in a number of Triple A appearances, he's yet to get his shot. He is trying to stay strong in his faith and confident in pursuing his dreams, but I know he's frustrated.

See, you don't *just* have to be good enough to get to the majors. So many other factors also have to align. Waivers. Rosters. Injuries. Trends in the game. Gaps on the team that need to be filled. It takes a lot of hard work, yes, but it also takes circumstances aligning. And before you know it, whether you've spent ten years in the majors or played ten games in them, eventually your body fails you and it's over.

Jake and I have had a number of conversations about how fleeting our idealized version of success really is. Sports are a poignant reflection of the way things work in life. A lot of minor leaguers are deeply in touch with the fleeting nature of success because of how hard they have to work to get where they want to go—and how easily all of it can slip away.

Perhaps you can relate. There is something in your life that you want. Something you have labored for out in the field whose fruit you have yet to see—or if you have seen it, were forced to reckon with how fleeting it was. But consider this: As you're laboring out in the field and planting seeds, is it possible there are inner workings of something you haven't expected, hidden beneath the surface?

Could you be reaping a harvest without knowing it?

Is something growing that you are blind to because of your idealized—and perhaps idolized—version of success?

For all the roller-coaster ride Jake's professional baseball journey has been, what we talk about most whenever the two of us meet are the lives he has seen changed through his relationships with guys in the dugout, his deep conversations with fellow players struggling in the minors, and all the moments that go far beyond his performance on the pitcher's mound. Those who would deem Jake a failure in his struggle to make the majors don't see his teammates being baptized, or witness the dugout prayers, or hear the late-night conversations in hotel rooms. Jake's journey has positioned him to relate more deeply to others in their own struggles and setbacks. It has developed patience and perspective within him. Commitment and compassion. Jake's journey has helped him think more clearly and feel more deeply.

WE ALL GET TO CHOOSE WHICH FRUIT WE WILL FOCUS ON: WHAT THE WORLD DEFINES AND ELEVATES AS FRUIT, OR THE FRUIT OF THE SPIRIT WITHIN US.

Sounds like a harvest to me.

We all get to choose whether we will bloom where we are planted.

We all get to choose whether we will dare to trust the inner workings of a mighty harvest happening beneath the surface.

We all get to choose which fruit we will focus on: what the world defines and elevates as fruit, or the fruit of the Spirit within us—love, joy, peace, patience, kindness, goodness, faithfulness, gentleness, and self-control (Galatians 5:22–23)—which will take us further in life than any accolade ever could.

▼ ▼ ▼

After the *Mike & Mike* show on my final morning at ESPN concluded, I turned in my laptop, iPhone, and iPad to one of my bosses, Kaitee, in the social media department. Then I said goodbye to Lisa, and that was it. I didn't make the rounds walking through campus, taking it all in, finding people and telling them goodbye, or anything like that. It might have made a better ending for a book if I had, but people were out of sorts. The date was February 10, 2017, and the day before, a bad snowstorm had torn through Bristol and forced a number of employees, including me, to work from home. So everyone was getting caught up on things before the weekend.

After saying goodbye to Lisa, I walked out of Building No. 5, where I had spent the majority of my seventeen years, and through the parking lot to my car. I started the motor and just sat there, looking out my frosted windshield at that brick building sitting there at the center of campus amid the layers of snow. I didn't cry; instead, I found myself overcome with appreciation. Defrosting my windshield forced me to slow down, and I thought about how I had spent seventeen of my forty-three years on earth at that wonderful place.

"Thank you, Lord," I said out loud. "I guess this is it."

ESPN had provided me with all kinds of wonderful memories and entertaining stories. But what I was most thankful for was that it had been the space I needed to become who I am today. It's where

I learned to wear the uniform of leadership. Learned to manage my ego. Learned to ask myself the hard questions, be content, live out my faith, and encourage others in theirs. Leaving ESPN was not how I expected my journey to unfold. For over a decade, I had all intentions of retiring there, given the opportunity. But I was trying to trust a narrative that had always been true for me on my journey: that the unexpected always brings the biggest results, and the risks that make me most vulnerable always lead to the greatest growth.

THE UNEXPECTED ALWAYS BRINGS THE BIGGEST RESULTS, AND THE RISKS THAT MAKE ME MOST VULNERABLE ALWAYS LEAD TO THE GREATEST GROWTH.

Two years after Jessica and Coach Dungy challenged me to bloom where I was planted, I was promoted to a senior manager position in the social media department. Some might see that as just a title, but I took it seriously. I never saw myself as a leader when I started working at ESPN. But seeing the words *senior* and *manager* side by side made me realize it was time to live out what I had learned. There would be opportunities to hire people, and opportunities to mentor them, and opportunities to do for others what people like Carol and Lisa and Bob and Gabe had done for me. ESPN taught me how to lead, perhaps the greatest gift one can ever receive. I was nervous about the next step, sitting there in my car on that snowy day, but I also felt confident and prepared. All because of the people at ESPN.

Directly after sharing the parable of the growing seed in Mark 4, Jesus shares the parable of the mustard seed: "What shall we say the kingdom of God is like, or what parable shall we use to describe it? It is like a mustard seed, which is the smallest of all seeds on earth. Yet when planted, it grows and becomes the largest of all garden plants, with such big branches that the birds can perch in its shade" (vv. 30–32).

I love how Jesus pointedly says the mustard seed is the smallest of all seeds. The most unexpected circumstances, the most unlikely conversations, the smallest displays of empathy, the tiniest outward-focused movements—all are a part of blooming wherever you are. All have purpose because they're part of the process of growing spiritual fruit. The seed might not look like much to the world. It might not seem like it will grow into anything special. It might not appear powerful at first. But God's kingdom is different from worldly kingdoms. Blooming is much different than the world's definition of success.

There is purpose behind the seed being planted. It grows, Jesus says, to become "the largest of all garden plants, with such big branches that the birds can perch in its shade." Our job is simply to do the work, like a faithful farmer, trusting the seed that is planted and knowing the rain will come and the process will unfold. We must let go of our expectations and find freedom in the process. It's about preparation and surrender. Everything else will take care of itself. It always does.

As the mustard seed's purpose in the parable was to provide branches for the birds to perch in its shade, so our purpose is to bloom for others. Wherever we are. However that looks. Your purpose as a leader is to be a simple seed that will grow and become a tree for others. A shelter where they feel safe and at rest. A sacred space for others to feel at home—so they, like birds, can fly and thrive.

PUTTING ON THE UNIFORM

No matter where you're at in your growth as a leader, remember that it's a process. You don't have to go from a seed today to a tree tomorrow. Maybe you feel you have yet to become that safe place for others to feel at home and to thrive beneath the canopy—that shaded space that helps others rest and gain strength so they can go out and fly once more. That's okay. Just keep trusting the process. Keep asking yourself the hard questions. Keep your mind in check. Keep your heart in check. Maintain your perspective. Be aware of the cultural narratives that tug at your soul. Be aware of the wants and needs of others. Be a leader who is marked by love, grace, and empathy. Strive to reflect those ideals, and the people you are leading will show you grace and empathy as well.

The daily pursuit of excellence is just that: a daily pursuit. You never quite arrive. That's what makes leadership fun. You are always growing as a leader, developing your culture, and evolving to meet the next generation where they are so you can come alongside them and help them unleash their own passions and desires. It is a beautiful, never-ending process.

So show yourself grace along the way. It's okay to slip back into old habits. (Just move on when you realize you've done so.) It's okay to make mistakes. Having grace for yourself will help you to have grace for others. Grace is the water that will help grow the seed of your leadership.

DISCUSSING THE UNIFORM

▷ What is the uniform of leadership to you? Think of a time when you wore it poorly and a time when you wore it well. What made the difference?

▷ What is true success to you? In what ways do you think the world's definition of success shapes your own? What changes can you make, both in your outlook and in practice, that could help you experience the kind of success described in this book?

CONCLUSION

A COUPLE OF WEEKS BEFORE we submitted the first draft of this book to the publisher, I received a call one evening from my boss, Howard, at Sports Spectrum. Though I have always had incredible bosses—at ESPN and Sports Spectrum—I think it's naturally human in today's culture to feel a twinge of fear when a boss calls you after hours. In the back of my mind, I wondered if I had done something wrong or left something important undone, or if there was a crisis of some sort.

"Hello?" I answered.

"Good evening, Jason," Howard said. "Hey, real quick, I don't want to take up much of your evening. But I wanted you to know that I just listened to your interview with Tenth Avenue North lead singer Mike Donehey on the *Sports Spectrum Podcast*, and I love this episode. It's one of your best. I just wanted to call you and quickly tell you how much I appreciate you and value your work. I'm so thankful you're a part of this company. You're doing awesome work, and I wanted to say thank you."

And that was it.

There was no agenda. No building me up in order to ask something else of me. No encouraging me in order to get to the truth of what he really wanted to say or to express criticism or frustration. No complaints. No projecting. No discouraging remarks or passive-aggressive jokes. The call did not create anxiety or brew fear. He just called to affirm and inspire.

Later that week, while grabbing lunch with one of my friends who had spent most of his career with a big insurance company, I told him about Howard's call. He looked at me and said, "In the twenty years I've worked for my boss, I've never received a call like that from anyone in leadership."

Think about that for a second. In twenty years of giving his time and energy to a company to help them move forward and meet their goals, no one had *ever* called him to encourage him or thank him for his efforts.

Want to know what the uniform of leadership is?

It's reflected in the call I received that evening. It's what Bob Ley did with *Outside the Lines* in attending every meeting and encouraging people in every level of the operation. It's what Carol Voronyak did with our team of talent producers in having us write thank-you notes to one another at Christmas, challenging us to find encouraging language for each person's unique gifts, talents, and contributions to the team. It's about Jennie Finch being so in touch with her own value and worth that it allowed her to affirm the value and worth of others. It's about Dale Earnhardt Jr. going the extra mile to show gratitude. It's about Drew Brees reaching the top but knowing there was still work to be done because excellence is a lifestyle, not a single thing to achieve. It's about Tony Dungy and his assistant, Jessica, inspiring an integrated life of body, soul, and spirit in the workplace. It's about Tami brightening her customers' mealtimes with warmth, care, and positivism in the cafeteria, day after day. I could go on and on.

THE UNIFORM OF LEADERSHIP ISN'T DIFFICULT TO UNDERSTAND, BUT IT IS PROFOUND AND COUNTERCULTURAL.

The uniform of leadership isn't difficult to understand, but it is profound and countercultural in a society that's so hyperfocused on performance, status, and worldly success.

If your family were sitting in the stands when you ran out onto the field in the first inning, would they see you wearing a uniform? If your coworkers were sitting in the stands, would they see your name or the name of your team on the front of your jersey? If God were sitting in the stands, what would he see when he looked past the lettering on your uniform and looked inside your heart?

Today maybe you're standing in the locker room and reevaluating your style of leadership. Maybe this book has challenged you or even agitated you at times, helping you see your own blind spots as I have shared my own with you. Take all the time you need in the locker room to deconstruct what didn't work before and reconstruct a different leadership style. Take the lessons in this book and build a style that will be inspiring to you and your team.

It's okay that you're not perfect. The people you are leading will give you grace in your imperfections if you're honest and vulnerable about your mistakes. One of the best things about leadership is that there is always something new to learn—and that means making a lot of mistakes. But don't forget that there is still a game to play, and it's never too late to lead in an inspiring, servant-focused way.

So grab that uniform and put it on. Know that you *belong* to something that is bigger than yourself. Know that you are *playing* for something that is bigger than yourself.

Now run through the tunnel out into the open, and be ready to love and serve like crazy.

Acknowledgments

There are many people who help put a book like this together, and just simply thanking them here would not do justice, but I would be remiss if I didn't say a huge thank-you to many of the people that helped make *The Uniform of Leadership* possible.

Thank you to everyone at Kregel for believing in me and our story. You are all amazing people to work with. I'm truly grateful.

Thank you to Stephen Copeland for being an incredible partner on this book. Your gift of storytelling is such a blessing to me and all those reading this book.

Thank you to David Shepherd for helping to find the right home for this story. Your guidance is something I am grateful for.

Thank you to my wife, Dawn, and my daughter, Sarah. I'm so thankful to have you two in my life. I love you both forever.

Thank you to ESPN for allowing me the honor to work for your company for seventeen years and accumulate so many amazing memories along the way. It truly was a dream job.

Thank you to my amazing coworkers at ESPN who invested in me and showed me what the uniform of leadership looked like on a daily basis.

Thank you to *you,* my readers, for taking the time to invest in this book. I pray it encourages you on your leadership journey.

To God be the glory.

Notes

1. Lexico, s.v. "uniform," accessed April 13, 2020, https://www.lexico.com/definition/uniform.
2. My two favorites are *The Carpenter* by Jon Gordon and *Lead . . . for God's Sake!* by Todd Gongwer. I highly recommend both books.
3. Jon Gordon, *The Carpenter: A Story About the Greatest Success Strategies of All* (Hoboken, NJ: Wiley, 2014), 25.
4. Darrin Gray and Hunter Smith, *The Jersey Effect: Beyond the World Championship* (Bloomington, IN: Westbow, 2012), 18–19.
5. Scott Van Pelt, "SVP's Heart-Warming Message to Long-time ESPN Employee: SC with SVP," ESPN, November 9, 2018, YouTube video, 2:32, https://www.youtube.com/watch?v=EdRWSU5b5QU.
6. Gordon, *The Carpenter*, 109.
7. Gordon, *The Carpenter*, 132.
8. Simon Sinek, "Why Good Leaders Make You Feel Safe," TED, March 2014, 11:47, https://www.ted.com/talks/simon_sinek_why_good_leaders_make_you_feel_safe.
9. Gordon, *The Carpenter*, 111.
10. Gordon, *The Carpenter*, 111.
11 Sinek, "Why Good Leaders Make You Feel Safe."
12. Jon Gordon, "True Grit," *Jon Gordon's Weekly Newsletter*, November 2, 2015, http://www.jongordon.com/positive-tip-true-grit.html.
13. Larry Bird, quoted in Michael Benson, *Winning Words:*

Classic Quotes from the World of Sports (Lanham, MD: Taylor Trade Publishing, 2008), 166.

14. Gordon, *The Carpenter*, 95.
15. Will Ferrell, "Will Ferrell Correspondent—Jim Rome Is Burning," Mike Reeder, July 6, 2014, YouTube video, 3:15, https://youtu.be/KsPWTnZgq7U.
16. "Mike and Mike Say Farewell to Producer Jason Romano," Jason Romano, March 22, 2017, YouTube video, 1:21, https://youtu.be/p7wU3CT-Oa4.

About the Author

Jason Romano is a speaker, author, media consultant, and church leader with twenty years of professional broadcasting experience on the regional and network levels. For seventeen years, Jason was a senior manager and producer at ESPN, where he produced content for several on-air television shows and ESPN Radio, helped lead and grow the talent producing department, and built relationships with the biggest names in sports. Jason is currently the host of the *Sports Spectrum Podcast*, an interview-driven show featuring stories on the intersection of sports and faith. Jason has spoken to thousands of people at conferences, colleges, companies, and churches over his career, and he looks forward to continuing his connections with sports fans and those called to lead.

Learn more about Jason at JasonRomano.com.